# Create Your
# Vision Board

## THE 2-HOUR GUIDE TO ATTRACTING
## THE LIFE YOU WANT

# MARCIA LAYTON TURNER

A POST HILL PRESS BOOK

ISBN: 978-1-68261-819-6
ISBN (eBook): 978-1-68261-820-2

Create Your Vision Board:
The 2-Hour Guide to Attracting the Life You Want
© 2018 by Marcia Layton Turner
All Rights Reserved

Cover design by Christian Bentulan

Post Hill Press, LLC
New York • Nashville
posthillpress.com

Published in the United States of America

# CONTENTS

*Putting what you want to do, be, or have in
visual form on a board helps your mind find
a path for you to achieve your goals.*
*Repeatedly viewing pictures and inspirational phrases
focuses your mind and triggers your unconscious to
attract new opportunities related to your goals.*

# INTRODUCTION

Beyoncé has one. Katy Perry has one. Deepak Chopra has one. Comedian Ellen DeGeneres, business mogul Oprah, and actor Jim Carrey even have them. I'm talking about vision boards, treasure maps, dream boards, or whatever term you want to use to describe a large piece of paper or bulletin board covered with pictures, photos, words, and inspirational messages describing your dream future.

"What's so special about a bunch of pictures and words?" you may wonder. What's special is that they have the power to change your life.

By creating a picture, or a collection of pictures, of what you want and then focusing your conscious and subconscious mind on it regularly, you can shape your future. Science has proven that we can train our brains to think differently, to learn new skills, and to attract new opportunities. You can do this with the help of a vision board.

You're about to learn how to create a tool that can attract almost anything you want when used regularly and properly. And it'll take you less than two hours to create one. So let's get started!

## How This Book Is Organized

This book is presented in four sections:

**Part 1, "Why Everyone Needs a Vision Board,"** explains exactly what a vision board is, why it is so powerful, and how it harnesses your mind to help you find ways to achieve your goals. You also learn about how the Law of Attraction works and hear success stories of people like you and me who have used vision boards to attract exactly what they wanted.

**Part 2, "Creating Your Own Vision Board,"** leads you through the basic process of setting goals, finding images that reflect those goals, and then designing a vision board to pursue those goals. Armed with your goals, paper, photos, illustrations, and meaningful words and phrases, you'll have the start of a terrific vision board in just a few minutes.

**Part 3, "Visions with a Purpose,"** is the section where you'll learn about many different kinds of vision boards. Here, you'll gain ideas and suggestions for the type of goals you might set and where to find pictures that reflect those desires, whether you're imagining yourself in a beautiful new home, cruising down the highway on a custom chopper, or traveling through Venice with your beloved partner.

**Part 4**, **"How to Use a Vision Board,"** deals with how to get results from that magnificent collage you just prepared. From dos and don'ts, to roadblocks, to various formats you can convert your vision board into, you'll learn more about tapping into these powerful tools.

**You will notice that, throughout the chapters, there are also success stories from vision board users to inspire you—results that people (including initial skeptics) had, thanks to their vision board.**

# PART 1

# Why Everyone Needs a Vision Board

Research has shown that being clear about your goals and committing them to paper can significantly increase the odds of achieving them. The Law of Attraction states that whatever you think about most, you will draw into your life. So how about focusing on the positive, enjoyable aspects of life? When you visualize your desires and transform them into something tangible, such as a vision board, your odds of success are even higher. Although they're fairly easy to create, vision boards can be powerful tools to harness your subconscious and conscious mind and to show you the path to attaining your goals.

# CHAPTER 1

# The Study of Vision Boards

Right now, are you living the life you always dreamed you would have? Do you have the home, the car, the bank account, the family, the lifestyle you pictured for yourself? If you do, you've clearly been living with intention and following your dreams effectively. But if you're among the rest of us—the majority—there are things in your life you'd like to change and improve.

This is where a vision board can help. Part goal-setting tool, part visualization technique, part focal point, a vision board helps clarify what you want out of life and then shows you how to get there—consciously and subconsciously. Made popular by the book *The Secret*, which talks in depth about the Law of Attraction, vision boards are powerful tools that can help you harness your energy to realize your goals and dreams.

## The Role of a Vision Board

Most people live week by week or month to month, focused on their short-term responsibilities, such as shuttling children to extracurricular activities, getting to work and back on time, hitting the grocery store because they ran out of milk last night, remembering to call a friend to wish him a happy birthday, paying the cable bill—you name it. Our lives can become filled with trivial tasks and obligations that obscure or distract us from our bigger dreams.

Fortunately, a vision board can help us refocus and remind us what is important. It can remind us of what we should and should not be doing in order to achieve our goals.

### Clarify Your Goals

Although the physical act of creating a vision board filled with beautiful pictures of how you'd like your life to be, complemented with affirmations and inspiring phrases, is fun, it's also a useful exercise to make sure you're on the right path.

Some experts recommend writing a personal purpose or life mission statement to guide your goal setting and vision board creation. This statement describes what you are on the earth to do. These are big-picture purposes, such as providing hope, helping others be the best they can be, or sowing peace.

By working on your own mission statement first, you may have an easier time preparing your life vision board.

By forcing yourself to seriously consider what you want your life to be like—what you want to do, be, and have—you then will know what kinds of photos and images belong on your vision board. Goal setting is what guides you to choose the pictures for your board that match your dream life.

## Focus Energy on Achieving Goals

Determining what your highest priorities are and then deciding you'll pursue them helps you to focus your energy on the activities with the highest values. Your highest priorities are those goals you paste onto your vision board.

By zeroing in on those experiences you want to have—the people you want to bring into your life, the creature comforts you desire, or the feelings of fulfillment and peace you long for, for example—you attract those opportunities. That's what a vision board does.

## Introduce and Reinforce New Habits

Vision boards can also be instrumental in introducing new habits into your life. By helping you decide what is most important to you, your vision board reminds you that you need to behave differently in order to have those experiences you desire.

You may have heard the joke that the definition of insanity is doing the same thing over and over and expecting different results. Well, a vision board helps you break those old habits by helping you focus on the changes you want to make in your life. Do you want to quit living paycheck to paycheck? Then you need to invest energy in holding on to your money longer. Want to take a vacation outside the United States? Start looking into where you would go and what you would need. Are you looking for your soulmate? Apparently, he or she isn't in the places you've been looking, so try a new social routine or group.

*Vision boards are very personal tools you can use to focus your energy on your highest goals and priorities.*

Looking at your vision board on a daily basis will help remind you of the new habits you've adopted and the changes you're manifesting.

Your mind processes pictures and photos much more readily than words and phrases, so frequently reflecting on the images on your vision board is an effective way to keep your goals in the front of your mind, literally.

## Encourage Action and Attract Opportunity

Some of the hoopla surrounding *The Secret* initially occurred because of some misinterpretation or miscommunication of the book's message. While vision boards can provide clarity about your goals, remind you of steps you need to take to make progress toward those goals, and attract new opportunities to lead you to success, vision boards will not cause things to magically materialize without any effort on your part. You need to act in order to make the most of your vision board; otherwise, it's just a wish board containing things you wish would happen, but for which you're not willing to work.

The real magic happens when you define, visualize, and capture your goals in one place—on a vision board—and then take steps toward realizing those goals. Your energy and action will work in concert and have the effect of attracting new opportunities that can lead to greater success.

By placing your goals on a vision board, you are communicating to everyone who sees it that these are your dreams and ambitions. The more people who see it, the more connected you become to new opportunities. Those new opportunities are exactly what will get you closer to your goals. Even if you keep your board private, though, your own energy invested in imaging your realized dreams can be enough to identify and attract those new opportunities for yourself.

Stephanie Bratter says, "For me, a vision board is just one small part of a life process," and that "it has certainly worked for me in terms of focus and manifesting intent into reality." She has many examples of success, with one being related to finances. Several years ago, the center of her board focused on prosperity. At the time, she was making two hundred dollars to five hundred dollars per month, but she put on the board that she would make at least two thousand dollars a month, added many dollar signs around it, and wrote, "I am a moneymaker." Today, she easily exceeds her two thousand dollar-minimum monthly income, mainly by keeping her vision board close by.

# Goal Setting 101

Before you can start to create an effective vision board—one that manifests the life you aspire to have—you first need to describe what that life looks like. Are you single, divorced, married, or in a relationship? Do you live in a farmhouse in the country, or are you in a penthouse suite overlooking the twinkling streetlights of Atlanta or the sparkling ocean on the coast of San Diego? Are you working at a job you love? Have you started your own business? Yes, before you can find pictures to represent your future life, you first need to decide what you want it to look like.

## What Is It You Want to Do, Be, or Have?

You'll learn all about the process of assessing where you are and where you want to be in Chapter 4, but to understand how a vision board works, you need to know that there must be thought and passion—energy—behind the images and words you put on your board. You need to feel a connection, a genuine desire to be that kind of person, to live that kind of life, or to have that particular item, in order for the vision board to do anything.

Simply putting pictures on a board may be entertaining, but unless the images resonate with you, they won't result in any noticeable change in you or your life. Seeing the images isn't enough; you need to feel in your bones what having those people or things or experiences in your life will feel like.

With the encouragement of his mother, Marla, teenager Ben Milling made a vision board early in his high school career. He wanted to graduate from high school.

According to school administrators and some of his teachers, that was a "reach" goal—one he was unlikely to achieve. Diagnosed with an intellectual disability, Ben had been told since first grade that he would never earn a real diploma—only a certificate of attendance. But that wasn't good enough for Ben.

He made a vision board with an image of a group of students wearing graduation caps and hung it his room. He wrote, "I am so happy to be graduating in June 2016," and attached clippings that read: "Achieve your dreams," "Anything is possible," and, "I can do it."

Teachers said he would never pass algebra, but with hard work, he did. He also got a job, which was a requirement for an Occupational Course of Study diploma. He worked the required 360 hours in high school, and he still has the same job more than four years later. Ben graduated in 2016 with his class, having earned a real high school diploma.

## What Will It Take to Get It?

The difference between looking at pretty pictures on a board and focusing on a vision board is that one board represents pictures of someone else, and the other represents your future. You need to feel hope, happiness, and optimism as you look at the images on your vision board in order for them to be yours one day.

The key to using your vision board to achieve your goals is to start with the end in mind—the life you want. You must then work backward to determine what types of actions you need to take, what kinds of people you need to meet, and what kinds of opportunities you need to be watching for.

# Tools for Goal Setting

Because just sitting down and trying to decide exactly how you'd like your life to be can be difficult, unless you've been asking yourself that very question for some time, you'll want to take a look at and try out some useful goal-setting tools.

### Five Years Hence

One tool, which is more like an exercise, is called Five Years Hence. Essentially, you need to imagine yourself five years from now—what you look like, what your life is like, where you live, where you work, what's important to you, and so on. You will then write that down, with as much detail as possible.

After you've clearly described your life five years from now, start to evaluate what you can begin to change in order to make that vision a reality. Do you need to change your diet? Start working out? Start saving more for that house you want? Quit hanging out at bars and check out professional networking meetings instead, or maybe try online dating? What do you need to start and stop to make strides toward your five-year goals?

## Mind Mapping

Another tool, which is great for breaking down big goals into smaller ones, is a *mind map*. Mind mapping is a technique for brainstorming new ideas, problem solving, and project management. By working from the center with an idea or a vision, you can then draw branches or paths that lead to several potential approaches, followed by increasingly detailed branches. Starting with a specific goal in the center, you can easily draw branches out to represent the many aspects of that goal and how you might pursue it.

By mind mapping your goals, you can create a visual road map to success. Working outward from your life's purpose or highest-priority goal, you can then identify supporting goals or actions—like an increasingly detailed to-do list. What makes the mind map so powerful is that, because it's visual and not a written list, it's easier for your brain to remember and process it.

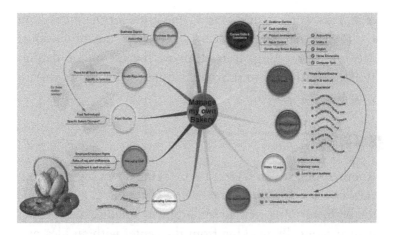

*Mind mapping is a great way to break down big goals
into smaller chunks and to identify pathways to achievement, step by step. (Image courtesy MindMeister.com.)*

## The Value of Clarity

Vision boards work. Whether by virtue of the Law of
Attraction, as some experts claim, or through achieving a clarity of purpose that leads to focused action, creating a vision
board has a very high probability of leading to improvements
in your life. That makes sense, because once you know what
you want with such clarity that you can point to a picture of
it, everything and everyone around you can be rallied to help
you attain it.

### Zeroing In on Success

Once you know that your biggest goal is to, say, get out of
a rented apartment and into a home you own—a home like
the one(s) you have carefully selected and pasted onto your

vision board—your brain becomes a filter, bringing relevant information and opportunities to your attention, while glossing over other, less important information. Your mind can behave like a homing beacon, guiding you closer and closer to opportunities to achieve success as you've defined it.

Whether your goal is to find a used washing machine costing less than a hundred dollars or a vintage designer dress to wear to the Oscars in the perfect shade of silver, after you train your brain what to be on the lookout for, you'll make quick progress.

Kathy Nelson created her first vision board back in 1977 in Seattle during a prosperity workshop. She put "San Diego Here I Come" on it with pictures of palm trees, beaches, and California, and hung it next to her front door so she could see it every time she came and went. "I didn't know how it might happen, just that I wanted to move to sunshine, the California lifestyle, and be closer to family," she explains. Along the way, her best friend decided she'd like to relocate to San Diego, too, and they became roommates. By August 1978, Kathy was following a U-Haul truck with her belongings down the coast to her new San Diego home. Two weeks later, she found a new career that led to a six-figure income.

## Easier Decision Making

Another benefit of clarity is that you can more quickly assess what opportunities fit the future you've visualized on your vision board. When you don't know where you're headed, it's harder to gauge which opportunities to pursue and which to let go. But when you know what kind of life you are working toward, deciding how to spend your money, your time, and your energy becomes so much easier and you see the results much faster, because you're not wasting as much time on inconsequential activities or diversions. Your vision board has painted a picture (or actually, you've painted the picture) of what you'd like, and now you can start working to match your current life to your vision of what's possible.

## Summary

- A vision board is a visual representation of how you would like your life to be.
- Recognizing what you want most in life is key to figuring out how to make changes.
- Your brain can process and remember pictures more easily than words, which is why a vision board is an effective tool for introducing new habits and goals.
- Once you know your highest priorities, it's much easier to identify potential pathways to success.

# CHAPTER 2

# Why Vision Boards Work

Although the process of creating a vision board sounds pretty simple—decide what you want, find pictures that represent that vision, and glue them onto a big slab of foam core—the activity can really change your life, because something inside you shifts when you become clear about your dreams. And when you start investing energy in making those dreams a reality, the world around you shifts.

Part of that shift is due to what some call the Law of Attraction, which states that whatever you think about or focus on you will attract. Another factor, however, is your brain's response. Neurologists have only recently started to discover that we can retrain our brains to think and react differently—the science is called *neuroplasticity*. Neuroplasticity is the study of the brain's ability to change, making new connections in response to environmental changes or injury.

By telling your brain what you want, it can then help you identify new patterns and connections to get you to your goals.

## Your Brain on Autopilot

Have you ever driven home from work or school and, because you've gone the same way a million times before, you can't recall much of the ride? Suddenly, you're in your driveway. That's how you've trained your brain to behave. You've approached many situations in this same way for years, training your brain how it should react. As a result, you've gotten what you've always gotten.

Fortunately, scientists are finding that you can train your brain to behave in new ways. With new responses and behavior patterns, you can uncover new possibilities, in terms of opportunities and performance.

### New Habits and Thoughts

The premise behind a vision board is that it can help you shift your focus from where you're headed now to where you really want to be. Using images, words, and numbers, you can push your brain to think about things other than what you normally think about. It may also prompt you to change your current behavior, so instead of getting sucked into hours of TV watching or web surfing, you might choose to go take a walk, call your mom, or browse a bookstore. Depending on what goals you've set for yourself, your vision board can raise your awareness of specific things you can do to improve your life.

Instead of your being reactive and letting the world lead you, your vision board can help you lead your own life. As you imagine how you can realize the dreams you've placed on your board, you may explore new ideas, new options, or new products, or meet people who can get you closer to your goals.

> Elizabeth Miller Gensler created her first vision board in 1994. At the time, she was launching a freelance career and searching for the perfect partner. In addition to career words and pictures, her vision board included a picture of a wedding dress with her head on top, a picture of a man and woman honeymooning on a beach, and other visuals depicting a romantic relationship. She established her freelance business within six weeks and met her future husband eighteen months later. Since then, she has used vision boards to help manifest serenity, an engagement ring, a home, a child, and her husband's growing biceps.

## Lather, Rinse, Repeat

Since your brain has been reacting the same way to new information, people, and situations for years, introducing new thought patterns can be challenging. If you've thought of yourself as a poor student forever, for example, shifting to thinking of yourself as gifted will be quite a shock to your brain. Your transformed reality may not happen overnight, but you'll move ahead more quickly if you stop the negative self-talk and doubt; and the images on your vision board can help with that considerably.

Whenever you find yourself questioning or skeptical of new information, stop and remind your brain of your new reality. Look at your vision board for reinforcement and then pat yourself on the back for being so successful.

The more you consciously change how you think about yourself, your environment, and your future prospects, the more quickly you'll see the items on your vision board materialize. That's because you've retrained your brain to look at the world differently—as a place filled with opportunities for successful people like you.

It's important to stick with those new patterns. Don't start to doubt yourself or return to old behaviors, or you'll get what you've always gotten—not enough.

## Picturing Your Future

In order to achieve the success you have envisioned, you need to transform your current life into the one you desire. That's what your vision board is designed to do—to show you what can be yours with applied focus and energy.

Five years ago, Gigi Langer decided to write a book about her recovery from addiction and created two vision boards to help ground her. The boards featured a number of images and phrases. She had a book with a shiny pink heart on the cover, which reminded her that the book would come from her heart and be filled with love. She attached the phrases "Create something good" and "Yes, you! You're done" to motivate her even when she felt discouraged. A white dove in flight holding a pink heart connected her to the power of creativity. And a photo of a woman leaping over a large round object was Gigi, overcoming all obstacles to achieve her goal. A photo of Oprah Winfrey gave her the courage to take the risk of penning a book.

Gigi looked at her vision boards daily, making progress on her book little by little. Then, in February 2018, *50 Ways to Worry Less Now: Reject Negative Thinking to Find Peace, Clarity, and Connection* was released, and it is a true testament to the power of vision boards.

## Repetition and Reminders

Since a vision board is a Law of Attraction tool, it makes sense that to achieve any kind of result, you need to spend time looking at your vision board and imagining your success. That's what the Law of Attraction indicates is required to attain the success you've pictured—repeated reflection on the words and images that describe your desired result. It is the frequent glances and daydreams about your board that will attract the very opportunities you need to achieve success. Constant attention and energy directed at your vision board will help you visualize your future so clearly, you can taste it. That's the key.

## Set It and Forget It

Of course, there's a fine line between working to change thought patterns and becoming obsessed. Spending too much time staring at your vision board is unproductive. Belief and confidence are also important here, and to a big extent you need to let go and allow the universe to take care of your future.

Once you've stated your intentions by creating a vision board featuring your desired life, reflect on it frequently to keep your mind focused, but don't act desperate. Your vision board is not something to be worshipped or prayed to—it's only a tool. Focus on what it will feel like when your son gets into his first-choice college, when you sell the home that's now too big, or when you retire to Fiji—whatever you're after. Won't that be fantastic?!

## The Power of Visualization

Do you ever feel like something is destined to be yours? Maybe it's a job you know you would be perfect for, an antique violin at an auction, or a dress to wear to an important upcoming event. There are instances in our lives when we are in total sync with something else—so in sync, almost on a cellular level, that we know instinctively it will be ours. That's the feeling that a vision board is designed to create within us. It helps create that connection to something or someone outside us. The result is that the opportunities come into our lives, not necessarily when or how we imagined, but typically they do come.

Katie Weber is a big believer in vision boards. Whenever she has a goal for herself, she creates a vision board for it and is "always astounded as the items on the board manifest." On her current vision board, she had a picture of a pair of diamond studs she wanted, but she was able to cross them off as received when her husband bought them for her, not knowing they were on her board. And that's only one of many items she has manifested with the help of vision boards.

## Summary

- Researchers have found that you can retrain your brain to approach situations differently, leading to new observations, behaviors, and opportunities.
- The Law of Attraction states that whatever you think about or focus on, you will attract.
- After introducing new habits and thought patterns, it's important to block doubt and self-criticism from your life, too.
- After you define your goals and set your intention for what you want to have happen, you need to believe. Ask and then believe, dictates the Law of Attraction.
- Visualizing a desired future is so powerful that the world's top athletes use it to train for their competitions. They study their environment—a snow-covered mountain, a balance beam, a swimming pool—and then they imagine themselves going down that mountain, doing somersaults

successfully on the beam, or finishing that final lap ahead of the other swimmers. They picture it over and over again with the same result—their winning. They train their brains to pursue and then achieve the success they desire. That's what you need to do to experience the success you desire.

# CHAPTER 3

# The Secret of *The Secret*

Until 2006, few people in the mainstream had heard of the Law of Attraction or *The Secret*. Released first in DVD and then in book form, Rhonda Byrne's *The Secret* became an overnight sensation by framing the Law of Attraction in a new light. Within a few short months, an estimated seven million copies of the book and DVD had been purchased. The message had clearly struck a chord.

In a nutshell, *The Secret* explains how what we think about most is what we draw into our lives. What we focus on and expect is what we get. Much like the adage "Success breeds success" or "Like attracts like," *The Secret*'s message is that a positive attitude and demeanor yield positive results. Conversely, a negative attitude—expecting the worst to happen—generally yields (the expected) poor results.

## Bringing the Law of Attraction to Light

Although *The Secret* provides a new take on the Law of Attraction, the information contained within its pages was far from new. The Law of Attraction has existed for centuries, some would argue, going as far back as to Abraham in biblical times. In more recent times, authors have written about attracting what we want into our lives, which is also called *manifesting.*

When you cause something to materialize by envisioning it and believing it will appear, you are manifesting. What you cause to come into your life is a manifestation. Whether it's a new job, the perfect mate, or that parking space right up front at the grocery store, what you attract, you have manifested.

### Preceding Works

Within the last century, several authors and scientists presented proof that the Law of Attraction was real and verifiable. Thomas Troward influenced the New Thought movement, which began around 1904 and suggested that brains can cause changes in an individual's environment, but the phrase "Law of Attraction" didn't emerge until it appeared in the works of William Quan Judge and Annie Besant in 1915 and 1919, respectively.

Later, in 1937, Napoleon Hill's book *Think and Grow Rich* crystallized much of what earlier thinkers and scientists had been arguing—that humans can change aspects of their lives through focused thought and visualization. Having sold more than sixty million copies, Hill's book is one of the best-selling books of all time and reflects the strong and ongoing interest in shaping our destinies.

*Think and Grow Rich* was one of the earliest books on the power of visualization and success.

## Why the Time Was Right

Still grieving and shaken by the terrorist attacks of 2001, Americans were moving on but were unsure of what their future held. The threat of more attacks loomed large, and many found it difficult to concentrate on anything but their own personal safety for months and years afterward. They were scared and emotionally stuck.

But *The Secret* gave readers hope that a happier, safer, more fulfilling future could be on its way. Its optimistic message gave readers the sense of control over their lives that had been lost a few years before, and Americans of all ages, religions, education levels, and income brackets raced to read it.

The idea that we as humans can shape our futures in such a way was riveting. After reading the book or watching the DVD, many individuals decided to take the next step, setting goals and creating vision boards to focus their energy and attention on what they truly wanted their lives to look like. *The Secret* was a catalyst that pushed many of us to figure out what was important to us and then to take action to make it happen. Those who read the book felt a confidence others lacked: that it really *could* happen.

*The Secret* rejuvenated our nation's interest in the Law of Attraction and highlighted the value of vision boards.

## Where The Secret Falls Short

Although *The Secret* spurred many people to define and work toward their ideal lives and lifestyles, critics have complained that it falls short in a number of areas. Few refute its basic principles, but some dispute several themes that seem to have come out of it.

First, many disagree with the book's focus on materialism and acquisitiveness. The Law of Attraction, at its core, is not meant as a delivery mechanism for things such as luxurious vacation homes, fancy sports cars, or boatloads of money. And yet, it can provide these things when the proper steps are taken. My sense is that these critics are merely disappointed that we're not thinking more broadly about the good that can be manifested, but few dispute that focus and action can yield what has been requested.

Perhaps a larger criticism is how easy *The Secret* makes goal attainment sound. The book suggests that you think about something you desire and *poof,* it arrives on your doorstep. Well, not exactly, the experts point out. There is work involved on your part and, depending on the complexity of your request to the universe, it could take days, months, or even years to achieve your goal—but that's not how it sounds in the book.

Other experts tear apart the book by pointing out claims the author makes that are not backed up or verified to any degree. Saying you have proof of something and actually demonstrating or documenting it are two totally different scenarios. Some say *The Secret* comes up a bit short on documented proof in a few cases, such as in detailing The Law of Attraction's historical roots or explaining how God fits into the equation.

Even though I concede these points and a few others people have made, nearly everyone who has studied the Law of Attraction agrees that it exists. You do have the power to make changes to your life that will bring you closer to attaining your goals—the trick is that you still need to take action. You can't just sit back on the couch and simply wish for your life to be better. You have to figure out how you want your life to be, picture it vividly, and then initiate change. Being able to picture it is where a vision board will help.

## Basic Tenets of Manifesting Goals

There are three components of manifestation—of bringing into your life what you most desire or changing your life for the better. These three steps make manifestation possible.

The three steps toward manifesting your goals, which are at the core of the Law of Attraction, are:

1. Determine your goal
2. Take action for change
3. Have faith

The first component, or step, of manifestation is that you need to determine what your goal is, or what your goals are. What are you striving toward? (This is where your vision board comes into play.) Then work backward to determine what critical steps are necessary to reach your goal. What is it that you need in order to succeed? Money? Connections? A plane ticket? Start to create your own mini road map to success.

Next, you need to take action. At this point, almost any action is progress, but you'll move most quickly toward achieving your goal if every action you take gets you closer to it. You need to prepare for your success, not sit back and wait for it.

So if your goal is to have some plastic surgery done, you might start by requesting information on the procedure you're considering. Or you could go online and find the names of cosmetic surgeons recommended by the American Board of Plastic Surgery. You might even schedule an initial consultation with a plastic surgeon to learn your options and get a recommended course of treatment. Stating your intention to get plastic surgery and gathering information is a big first step toward attaining your goal.

Finally, you need to have faith. You need to believe you are on the path to success, to achieving your goal, even when you may see no physical evidence of progress. Believing is critical. There is no room for skepticism or disbelief.

Author Peggy McColl did more than wish that her book *Your Destiny Switch* would become a *New York Times* bestseller—she created mini vision boards that reflected its coming bestseller status. McColl found a book with a *New York Times* bestseller sticker on the cover, cut it out, and pasted it on the cover of *Your Destiny Switch*. Then she made color copies of the book's cover and placed them all over her house on practically every surface. So when her book made the *New York Times* list soon thereafter, it wasn't a complete surprise, even though it was certainly a joyful accomplishment.

If you start to feel you're not making progress fast enough, you may be overlooking important changes in your outlook or attitude that have occurred. Don't beat yourself up or become depressed about the speed at which your goals are being realized. Keep working at them.

The Law of Attraction is what propels you toward your goals, but a vision board is the tool you use to stay on track.

## Summary

- Although the Law of Attraction has become a more commonly heard concept in recent years, its origins date back to biblical times.
- Be as specific as possible when selecting images to focus on—too general a picture and you may be surprised by what you end up with.
- Until you know what you want for yourself and others, you can't concentrate fully on imagining that reality.
- In addition to creating a board that visually reflects your dreamed-of future, it is also important to focus on the feeling—the sensation—of having achieved that goal.
- Modern science has proven that the brain can change in response to what's in our environment or to new physical limitations caused by an illness or injury.
- Focusing your brainpower on a vision board can actually stimulate changes and additional neuron activity within your brain that lead to new insights and opportunities.

# PART 2

# Creating Your Own Vision Board

Although it may look like a simple board covered with images and words, a vision board is actually created through a process that reflects what you most want to draw into your life.

Starting with some goal-setting exercises to clarify your hopes and dreams, you can then begin to seek out photos, illustrations, and phrases that reflect and reinforce what you're working toward. For some, that might be a new car or a trip abroad, while for others it might be patience and harmony. Your vision board provides a focal point for your goals and ambitions.

# CHAPTER 4

# What Do You Want?

Now that you understand the basics of the Law of Attraction and why and how it works, it's time to start figuring out what you want. Once you know that, you can start creating a vision board that reflects your dreams and ambitions.

Your first step is to do some self-reflection and goal setting so that your vision board can help you attain those short- and long-term goals. Until you're clear about how you'd like your life to be different, it'll be tough to find images that lead you in that direction. Choosing that direction is what this chapter is all about.

# Setting Life Goals

Remember back in high school when someone—probably an adviser or a guidance counselor—asked you what you wanted to be when you grew up? If you were like most people, you probably had little idea what career you intended to pursue. Should you be a lawyer, doctor, ballplayer, stay-at-home mom, teacher, artist, chef? Only the most self-aware individuals who had really stepped back and evaluated their interests and skills could probably answer that question without the assistance of a personality or skills test. Until you've evaluated where you've been, what you've liked, and where you want to go, it's hard to choose a path forward.

Well, now you have a chance for a do-over. You're presumably out of high school, and now I'm asking you, what kind of life do you want for yourself?

## What Are You Good At?

The best way to start planning your future is to look at your past. What makes you special? What do people frequently compliment you on? What are you really good at—better than 95 percent of the population? Or, what do you know more about than everyone else? These are your strengths.

Before you can set goals for yourself, it's important to be sure they are relevant. That is, are these dreams, goals, or targets things that make you jump out of bed in the morning? Are they significant? Are they exciting to you? Can you see yourself playing a certain role or living a particular kind of life? If they don't excite you, then they're someone else's goals—not yours.

Keep in mind that what you're best at may have absolutely nothing to do with your current career or job. Dig deep to remember what you loved doing as a child, what your career aspirations were back then, and what you dreamed of becoming when you were older. Those types of activities and goals are useful to remember because they represent what you truly loved to do before anyone started pointing you toward or away from a certain career path or lifestyle.

What really makes you light up may be a hobby, like sewing or hang-gliding. Maybe it's speaking to local youth groups or volunteering at your place of worship. Or it could just be teaching your child how to swim or to read.

So start by making a list of your strengths—what you're good at and what you love:

- Learned skills—such as playing a musical instrument, speaking a foreign language, or designing websites
- Innate talents—such as playing a particular sport, performing mathematical calculations, or possessing a superior sense of smell
- Hobbies—such as sailing, playing fantasy football, or writing poetry
- Personality traits—such as a sense of humor, diplomacy, persuasiveness, confidence, or initiative
- Communication skills—such as public speaking skills, writing ability, or social skills

What you excel at—whatever it may be—is key to what you should be doing. It's a sign pointing to how you should be spending much of your time. These are the kinds of activities and pastimes that you'll want to consider including on your vision board to attract opportunities to engage in them more frequently.

## What Is Important to You?

Of course, if what you're good at isn't important to you and you don't enjoy it, it's irrelevant. To help find the intersection of what you're good at and what is important to you, make another list. What types of activities would you never give up?

- Volunteer work—such as counseling, fundraising, or sitting on an advisory board of directors
- Fitness-related activities—such as working out with a personal trainer, doing gym workouts, or exercising outdoors
- Family obligations and events—such as attending teacher meetings, concerts, and children's extra-curricular activities
- Getaways—such as summer vacations, family reunions, and weekend outings
- Studying and learning—such as pursuing continuing education, working toward a college degree, or participating in online learning
- Creative activities—such as theatrical programs, artistic outlets, or crafting

Richard Warren created his first vision board in 1993, thanks to a friend who offered instruction and free pizza to those willing to come and make one. Richard cut out pictures from magazines of what he wanted and pasted them onto the board, still somewhat skeptical of the process. But he hung it in a location where he would see it daily, at his friend's urging. More than a year later, something made him stop and take a good look at the board, which he had all but ignored. To his astonishment, he had achieved eight of the ten goals on the vision board. Every year since then, he has prepared a new vision board, "with fantastic results," he says.

In addition to how you spend your time, are there personal possessions you hold dear? Perhaps things you dream of owning or having?

- A new car
- A new house
- A romantic partner
- Children of your own
- A vacation spot or second home
- Pets
- Jewelry
- Higher education for your children
- Sports vehicles
- A nonprofit foundation established for a personal cause

Think through what you want your life to consist of and what you want in it. As you picture your dream life, you'll catch glimpses of pieces of the puzzle that you'll want to make sure are on your vision board.

## What Is Your Life Mission?

Some people have a long list of material things they desire, while others are less interested in things and more inclined to work toward the greater good. That's not to say we're all not working toward the greater good in some shape or form, but it's a matter of degree. If having a new car or big, well-appointed home isn't at the top of your must-have list, perhaps you're more focused on making a difference in the lives of others.

Whether you enjoy material pleasures or not, it can be worthwhile to consider why you're here on earth. If you have a personal mission or purpose, what is it? Some people believe that we all have a purpose we are trying to fulfill—a purpose that might be feeding the hungry, educating the illiterate, housing the homeless, and so on. There are an infinite number of possible life purposes. Whatever your purpose, it can give you fulfillment and satisfaction that no product can.

Once you determine yours, you may want to reflect that on your vision board. Whatever your life purpose is, it is likely to impact how you spend your time, what your bigger life goals are, and more.

## What Does Your Future Hold?

Given what you recognize now about your strengths and weaknesses, interests, desires, and life's purpose, what does your future look like? What does a typical day hold for you?

Where do you spend most of your time? Whom do you spend time with? How do you look and feel?

This vision of your life is what your vision board should reflect—that happiness, satisfaction, and sense of peace.

## Long-Term Goals

Now that you have a general sense of where you're headed, you can start to lay down some specific long-term goals. These goals should be at least five years in the future and be things, experiences, or achievements you are striving for. The more specific the goals, the better you'll be able to recognize opportunities for progress.

### Financial

One of the most prominent goals we all set is financial in nature. In five to ten years, how much will you be making, what will be your net worth, what will your portfolio be worth, will all your student loans or mortgage be paid off, or what kind of assets will you have attained? These are all long-term questions you'll want to ask yourself as you picture your financial health several years hence.

What's great about financial goals is that they are quantitative and specific. That is, they consist of numbers. Although some goals can be wishy-washy, such as, "I want to become more patient," or "I want to be promoted," financial targets can't help but be specific. As a result, they are measurable, so you can easily track how well you're doing on your path to reaching your goals.

So where do you expect to be five years from now financially? Will you have paid off all your credit-card debt? Will you be earning 20 percent more? How about ten or fifteen years from now? Will you have saved enough for your child's college education? What are the milestones you've mentally set for your financial goals? Set them and then start thinking about what kind of pictures represent them so you can place them on your vision board.

## Relationships

While we don't always appreciate the people around us, the fact is that family and friends probably have the biggest impact on our happiness—more than money, fame, or material objects. Improving your relationships with people in your life now and consciously looking for relationships that you lack have the power to transform your life.

Long term, you may try to change your relationships with those around you by reducing the negative exchanges that occur—either caused by you or by them—and increasing the positive, pleasant experiences you have. Think about what you can do to make that shift.

When you hear the term "relationship," you probably picture a romantic bond. If one of your long-term goals is to get into a new romantic relationship, it's time to get clear about with whom. What does he (or she) look like? What are his best traits? What does he like to do? And, most important, how does he act and make you feel? Make a list of your desired partner's traits so you can recognize him when he comes into your life.

## Spiritual

Americans have become much less religious in the past few decades. Many have left their faith behind. If you are in that group and want to reconnect with God or your higher power, how about setting some goals for how that can happen?

Do you need to find a new place of worship? Do you need to start following a more spiritual path, perhaps in the form of service to others? Or do you intend to add spiritual acts on a daily basis, such as prayer before meals or bedtime? Picture your day as a more spiritual person. Those are the types of images you'll want to find and feature on your vision board.

## Health

If a change in your health is what you're working toward long term, be as clear as possible about what you want and how you'll get there. Do you want a sleeker physique? Do you want to ward off potential disabilities? Do you want to end pain in certain parts of your body?

When you're clear about where you're headed, you can start evaluating what will get you there. Your new health regimen may involve a change in your diet, a new exercise routine or schedule, or adding a new medical routine such as massage or chiropractic to your body-care program. Consider where you want to be health-wise in five or ten years and anticipate new challenges you may face as you age, then look for pictures that reflect your best you.

## Career or Business

Although we probably don't set health goals as often as we should, setting career or business goals is much more common. Some corporations expect it as part of an annual performance review, while business owners are often forced to do it just before tax time. Too frequently, though, that type of planning looks just one year out. What does your long-term career plan look like? If you're an entrepreneur, where will your business be in five or ten years?

As you picture your desired position several years hence, what kind of job are you in? What title do you hold? Do you supervise others? Have your own expense account? Hobnob with the senior execs, or are you one? Or maybe you've retired and are enjoying your free time.

If you're a business owner, are you still running the place or have you turned it over to someone else? How are sales? Are there new markets you've entered, or do you offer new products or services? What is the state of your company?

## Hobbies and Outside Interests

If what you're passionate about has nothing to do with your full-time job or how you spend your days, it's time to fast-forward several years and picture yourself with respect to your hobby or pastime. Are you spending more time on your hobby? Have you achieved some level of recognition? Are you making money from it? Have you received opportunities to meet some of the industry's leaders?

How would you like your hobby to be a part of your life in five or ten years? Picture that and then find some images that reflect your involvement with that pastime for your vision board.

Although creating a vision board is typically a very personal activity, it can also work for organizations. 1-800-GOT-JUNK? uses a "Can You Imagine?" wall to inspire employees to think big. Some of the accomplishments that have resulted from the vision board wall include having a quote from the company's CEO on a Starbucks cup, having 1-800-GOT-JUNK? included in a Harvard Business School case study, and being featured on *Dr. Phil.* "We find that dreaming big and putting those dreams out there, where other people can read them, helps to make them happen," says Shaye Hoobanoff, the company's PR manager.

## Short-Term Goals

While we often tend to think short term, long-term goals are often easier to define, because almost anything is possible five or ten years in the future. You could be married, fifty pounds thinner, or running a multimillion-dollar company based on a loved hobby—but what about next month or next week? What goal can you set and achieve for yourself in that time frame? That may be a little tougher to zero in on.

### Financial

Long term, you want to be wealthy with zero debt, but what can you do between now and next week to get on that path? What steps can you take to improve your personal financial condition? Are there behaviors you can start, such as setting aside 5 or 10 percent of your paycheck in a new bank account? Or behaviors you can stop, like going out to lunch every single workday?

Start slow so you don't burn out too quickly, such as by setting up a savings account or bringing lunch to work once the first week and two times the next week or next month. Change can be gradual, but you need to start identifying how you're going to make it. That's the short-term challenge, and figuring that out will help you find pictures and phrases to add to your vision board to spur you on.

## Relationships

You can't overhaul your family dynamics overnight, nor can you stop your best friend from talking about her new baby incessantly, but you can identify what you are going to do to make those relationships more satisfying for you.

Are there things you can do more often to please your family members, like stopping by or inviting them over for a nice dinner? Maybe your friends just want to see you more often, without your new beau or husband. Or maybe they all just want you to show up on time for once.

What is it that you can do right now to please someone who is important to you? Figure that out, decide you'll try it, and then consider adding it to your vision board in picture form to remind yourself of that change you're making.

## Spiritual

Changing your spiritual path is also a step-by-step process. What exactly do you want to change about your relationship with God? You need to know that first, and then you can think about what you can do to improve it.

Do you need to attend worship services more often? Do you need to become more active at your temple? How about participating in more community service projects? Spirituality can be reflected in so many ways, so determine first what change you want to make and then find pictures showing those changes in place.

## Health

As with anything, you may want to completely reverse the poor health habits you've grown into over the past few years, but it can't happen overnight. You need to start slowly and build up to activities that will improve your long-term health.

So what can you do today to be healthier? Will you eat one more serving of vegetables? Smoke two fewer cigarettes? Take the stairs once during the day at work? Get to bed before 1:00 A.M.? Figure out what one thing you can start today that will make the biggest impact on your health, and then in a few days, add another healthy step. Find pictures and inspiring words that will keep you on that healthy path so you can achieve that long-term image of your healthier self.

## Career or Business

At work, it may be harder to distinguish what you can do immediately to impress your boss or bring in more customers to your business, but if you take a few minutes to review what you know your boss or your customers like to experience in terms of behavior, you will certainly be able to come up with a few short-term changes.

Maybe you'll arrive earlier to work or stay later, speak up more in meetings, or speak less to your colleagues during work hours. In your business, maybe you'll pick up the phone to check in with your best customers, get their orders out a day early, or design a new promotion that you know they'll love. Decide what behaviors you'll change and then draw or find illustrations or pictures you can use on your vision board to reinforce these positive changes.

## Hobbies and Outside Interests

You may have big long-term goals for turning your hobbies into a full-time income stream, or maybe you just want a few extra minutes each day to catch up on the latest sports news, if that's your passion, or to draw, read, or quilt, for example. What changes would you like to make in your life that would allow more time for your hobbies?

As you picture what you could do differently to carve out this important time, also imagine how you'll use the time to create, relax, or engage in your favorite pastime. Could you clean out a corner of a room and claim it for your jewelry making? Could you put the kids to bed fifteen minutes earlier or get up fifteen minutes before they do to have some time to enjoy your activity? Decide what you can do tomorrow to make time for what you love, and then find a picture for your board that shows it working well for you.

# Breaking Down Big Goals

Whether you're thinking long term or short term, tackling a major goal is scary. How will you get from point A to point B?! When you first look at a massive goal, it can be daunting. You may have all the confidence in the world about your abilities, but until you can make a road map, you can't be successful.

That's what your vision board can help you do, both consciously and subconsciously. By putting your goal on the board—your point B—you're helping your brain imagine where you're headed, almost like a GPS. But you can also help it get on course more quickly by breaking that major task down into more manageable chunks. By finding and adding pictures of those milestones to your vision board, you'll hasten your success.

## Working Backward

One of my favorite planning tactics is to work backward from my goal. For example, if I know I need to lose forty pounds before my high school reunion next June, I can figure out how much I need to lose per month or per week to hit that target. Then I can design a diet and workout routine to get me there. My vision board would include pictures of that diet and routine to reinforce what I'm doing to achieve success.

Working backward works for nearly any kind of activity or goal, such as earning a degree, completing a project, renovating a home, planning a vacation, saving for a new-car down payment, or building traffic to a new website.

## Annual, Monthly, and Weekly Goals

Depending on your time frame for reaching your goal, you may plan in terms of an annual target or maybe monthly or weekly targets. If you're setting income goals, annual ones may be more effective, because you may not be able to immediately grant yourself a salary increase. But if you're working on saving money, volunteering your time to a favorite cause, or working out, weekly or monthly goals may be a better way to track your progress. When you track yourself more frequently, you have more opportunities to change course if things aren't improving as quickly as you wanted.

Find images of those milestones to glue to your board to remind yourself that this is a process, not an overnight event. You can do it.

## Fifteen-Minute Increments

If you can, break down those goals even further, into fifteen-minute increments. The more specific you can be about what you need to do on a daily basis, the less likely you are to fall back into your old routine.

So if you want to travel to Italy next year, let's say, a number of things need to occur. Find a photo of where you want to go in Italy first, to remind you of your goal, and place it on your board. Then identify all the steps you need to take to make it happen.

For example, you need to get the money to pay for the trip, set aside the vacation time, get a passport, arrange for pet sitters, plan your travels once there, and so on. Work on that list, and when you're confident it's fairly complete, break each major step down and then break it down again until you have something you can do in less than fifteen minutes.

To get a passport, for example, your fifteen-minute step tomorrow might be to go online and find out what you need in order to get one. The next day your fifteen-minute step might be to find a place that takes passport photos and schedule an appointment, and so on.

As you identify all the steps, put pictures on your vision board, and as you accomplish them you can either check them off or remove them from the board so your brain doesn't have to work on helping you complete them anymore.

## Summary

- Setting goals for how you want your life to be will help you see the changes you need to make.
- Sometimes taking the long-term view first can be helpful in figuring out what you want for yourself.
- Once you've clarified where you're headed, it's time to bring the focus closer to the present with short-term goals.
- Armed with short-term goals, break them down even further into fifteen-minute steps so you can reap immediate results.

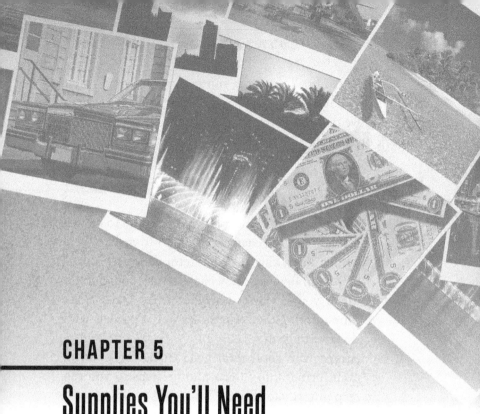

# CHAPTER 5

# Supplies You'll Need

A vision board is a tangible, physical reflection of how you would like your life to be. It's a collage, really, of your desired life. Creating your own vision board involves turning thoughts of what you desire into pictures of what that life will be like when you achieve it. In doing that, you help your brain imagine and feel what it will be like when you achieve your goal.

The first step in creating a vision board is to gather the components you'll need. The basics are a board, images, quotes or special sayings, scissors, adhesive to make them all fit together, and a frame so you can hang your board. It's actually a very fun activity!

## Your Vision's Foundation

Since you will be applying photos and pieces of paper to your board, I recommend using something sturdy, rather than standard white copy paper. You want a board that is going to stand up over time, that you can easily move without destroying, and that has some weight.

Most people feel more positively or are more impressed by information presented on heavier, weightier paper, rather than the flimsy stuff. Kinesthetically it feels more substantial so, as a result, they take whatever is on the paper—a résumé, proposal, or presentation—more seriously. This is one of the reasons why you should use a stocky board for this important project.

The size and shape of your board, the backing for your vision board, can be as large or small as you like. Many vision boards are poster-sized, eighteen by twenty-four inches or so, in order to fit multiple images and goals, but yours doesn't have to be. You can choose to make a more compact vision board that fits into an eight-by-ten-inch frame, for example.

In addition to considering how many images you have to display or goals you want to address, also think about where you plan to hang or place your vision board. How much wall or furniture surface do you have? You might want to scale back a smidgen if you have only one cubicle wall at work, for example, or if you want to be able to carry your board with you inside your notebook. We'll talk about portability later, but for now, mainly think about where you're going to keep your vision board.

## Foam Core

The most popular board used for vision boards is foam core, which is also commonly used for mounting photos and artwork. Foam core is a strong but lightweight cardboard-like material consisting of about one-quarter inch of Styrofoam sandwiched between coated paper. It is available in many colors and sizes.

You can quickly and easily cut down foam core with a sharp X-Acto knife, too, if you decide you want a smaller vision board.

## Poster Board

Many people opt to apply their vision—their words and pictures—to poster board because it is inexpensive, easy to find, and easy to use. You can cut it with scissors and even adhere it to another surface should you decide you want a firmer backing.

The only real downside of poster board is its thickness. It's thinner than foam core, which makes it easier to roll up and carry, but that also means it can't stand up on its own. You can apply images to it using glue and rubber cement, which is good, but you can't use tools such as T-pins or push-pins on poster board, because they would break through to the other side.

## Corkboard

Although most people tend to glue their photos and information to backing, that's not a requirement. You can just as easily tack a picture onto a cork or bulletin board by using pushpins. In fact, not having the images permanently adhered makes it easier to adjust or move them, or to remove them when you achieve your goal.

You can buy cork squares with adhesive backing or cork used for flooring, or you can take the easy route and buy a prepared bulletin board complete with a frame. (I'd take the easy route, personally.)

Krysia Hepatica was a newly-divorced single mom going to school full time, with big goals and plans. Money was tight, but she knew it would get better.

She made a vision board on a corkboard, filling it with images of what she wanted to attract: "new career, friends, happy times with my kids, outdoor recreation, and travel," she says.

"I found images of everything I wanted to attract in my mom's old magazines and some product catalogs from the REI store I was working at. To represent travel, I cut out a picture of a suitcase I found," she says.

"I often looked at the life I was trying to manifest on that board, and everything I wanted, I eventually received."

In fact, about a year after creating the board, she ended up getting the exact suitcase she had put on her board "at a fraction of the price because of a special sale open to employees only—I needed a bag to take with me on my trip to Paris!"

## Canvas

Similar to the corkboard, you could also use a blank fabric canvas. This is smart if you intend to paint some of your own imagery on the board. But even if you're not planning to paint, a stretched canvas allows you to either glue or pin images to it.

The type of board surface you choose to use will have no real impact on how quickly you achieve your vision or reach your goals. What's most important is finding a surface you can place images and words on that can then be viewed regularly. The frequency with which you look at your vision board will have a much bigger impact than whether you choose foam core or poster board! Don't overthink it.

## Images

When you're armed with your empty board, it's time to start gathering images to apply. Before you begin placing them, you should have described your life vision and created a list of the types of pictures or drawings that show it as you'd like it to be (see Chapter 1 for help with goal setting). That is, don't just start cutting, taking, or drawing pictures without having done the groundwork to decide what you want on your board.

## Taking Your Own Photos

One of the easiest ways to get pictures for your board is to take them yourself or unearth them from photo albums you already have. This can be especially helpful if, for example, you want to show yourself a few years ago with a different hairstyle or without the baby weight, or if you want to show that house on the beach you rented last summer and would like to visit again.

The benefit of photos you've taken is that they can help you recall when the picture was taken—how you felt, who was there, or what you were doing. Those details can boost the effectiveness of your vision board by helping you imagine yourself as having already achieved your goal.

But don't limit yourself to existing photos—taking new ones of places, situations, and things you want in your life, rather than just pulling from a magazine, can really bring your board to life. From snapshots of your best friends to panoramic photos of the park where you want to be married, photos you take yourself can make the goals clearer.

Whether you take photos with a traditional film camera or a digital camera really doesn't matter, because what you need for your board is the prints, the output. If you don't have your own camera, you could buy an inexpensive disposable camera or borrow a friend's or family member's camera.

You have a number of options for getting your photos printed. You can have them printed by the photo-processing department of a local department, grocery, or drug store. You can upload them to an online photo processor such as Shutterfly or Snapfish and have prints mailed to you (look for an online discount code first). Or you can print them out on a color inkjet or laser printer, if you have access to one.

Another benefit of using photos you've taken yourself is that you can edit and crop them to fit your needs. Want to zoom in or touch up a photo? It's easy to do when you own it or have access to it, but not as easy when it's a magazine cutout.

## Magazines and Books

Of course, magazines and books are terrific sources of beautiful, inspiring images. Whether you're in search of an image of a luxury automobile, a skier gliding down a mountain, or a perfectly kept home office, you'll likely be able to find it within the pages of a magazine or an illustrated book.

A number of years ago, James Roche (www.infoproductguy.com) of Miami Beach, Florida, made a vision board that included a couple of photos of the type of woman he wanted to attract into his life. He knew what he wanted—a woman with a certain look, intelligence, and culture about her. Within four months of putting together his vision board, he attracted exactly the type of woman he was looking for. They are now happily married.

The great thing about magazines is that there are so many of them. In fact, no matter what kind of photo or illustration you're hunting for, there is probably a magazine devoted to it.

Looking for a shot of the latest luxury motorboat? Track down a copy of *Powerboat* magazine, and you should have plenty of photos to choose from. Aiming to create a soothing, organized home? *Real Simple* is probably just the ticket. In need of a photo of a healthy but slim woman to serve as your weight-loss role model? Publications like *Health* and *Runner's World* are just what you need.

Although you can certainly head to your local bookstore to stock up on the latest magazine issues, it's not hard to find back issues at no cost. The best places to look are at area recycling operations or library magazine exchanges. You can also photocopy photos from magazine issues you borrow from the library, but cutting from the glossy pages is more fun.

Magazines are the most common source of photos, but books are another great source for photos and illustrations. You might have an easier time finding historic photos in a book, for example.

If you find just what you need in a book, head to a website like PaperBackSwap.com to trade for it at no cost. Or try and pick it up used for less at Half Price Books (www.hpb. com) or your local used-book store. Again, you can also photocopy borrowed books to save yourself some money.

## Clip Art

If you don't mind perusing images on a computer screen, rather than on pages, clip art may be an excellent source. Clip art is artwork—simple illustrations, drawings, computer-generated imagery, cartoons, and photos—that is available for anyone to use. You can buy clip art software packages, or you can download images directly from clip art websites, sometimes for a fee.

The only real downside to clip art is that it is often generic, designed to be able to illustrate a wide variety of texts and materials. On the other hand, you can quickly search hundreds of thousands of images to find something that is close enough to what you're looking for, such as a swimming pool or college diploma, to reflect your goal.

You can find clip art on websites like Clipart.com, where, for a small fee, you gain access to hundreds of thousands of images. Or you can buy a software package at an office supply store that contains a huge database of images for less than fifty dollars. However, there are also websites that provide clip art at no charge. Try a Google search for "free clip art" to find free sources.

Other popular sources for clip art include:

- 1ClipArt.com
- Free-Clip-Art.com
- HassleFreeClipart.com

## Travel Guides

If traveling the world, or just visiting a specific destination, is part of your vision for yourself, travel guides produced by travel agencies, countries, cruise lines, or specific resorts can be a terrific resource for your vision board.

The images are always professionally taken and reflect the very best view of the location. The only photos that would be better than the ones in professional travel guides would be photos you took on a previous trip there—because they help you remember the experience.

Samantha Siffring is no stranger to vision boards. She has made several and has found that "even when I set them aside and forget about them for a while, when I come back to them, I've accomplished or gained so much of what I find on them!"

Last year, as part of her intention to do some traveling, she cut out photos from travel magazines. She "chose this gorgeous photo of a lake with mountains in the background" as her central image—as a scene she'd like to see and experience. After adhering it to her board, she saw that it was Lake Josephine, and she felt a connection to it since her daughter's middle name is Josephine.

Intrigued by that connection, Samantha began making conscious plans to visit the area and to hike Lake Josephine. A year later, she and her family took a road trip to Glacier National Park and hiked to the lake. "It was surreal to stand at the banks of the lake and remember putting it on my vision board a year before," she says.

## College Catalogs

Sometimes what we envision for our future has more to do with our family, and especially with our children or grand-children, than ourselves. If one of your goals is for your child or children to attend college—perhaps even a specific college or university—why not request a college catalog and use images from it on your board?

Or maybe one of your goals has been to go back to school and earn that college or graduate degree you've always wanted.

## Online Images

If one or more of your goals is a bit more obscure and images of it are not likely found in a college catalog or magazine, hop on the internet and do a Google search to try to track down just the right photo or illustration. It's best if you have the capability to print the image in color, because it's more realistic.

Other good sources of online images include:

- Wikimedia Commons
- Pinterest
- FreeImages.com
- Shutterstock
- Getty Images

## Draw or Paint Your Own

Yet another option is to create your own images, either directly on the board or on a piece of paper that you then place on the board.

# Words and Quotes

Alongside those colorful visual images of your future life, you may decide to use some words and phrases to reinforce the success you're aiming for. These may be quotes that inspire you, words that express your goals, or meaningful phrases that encourage you.

Is one of your goals to obtain a certain dollar amount? Actor Jim Carrey wrote himself a ten million-dollar check when he was struggling, in order to stay focused on what he was truly worth as an actor and where he was headed. Today he earns at least that per film. If you'd like to print out your own check to fill in your desired amount, go here:

www.whatisthesecret.tv/the-secret-scrolls/the-secret-check.html

## Online Sources

Of course, the easiest source of quotations and verbiage is you! If you have catchphrases or goals you want to have on your vision board, you can simply type them up on your computer and print them out. No need to go looking for them if you already know what they are.

But if you feel you need some more inspiration or encouragement than you currently have for your board, there are a number of websites you can turn to for ideas. Here are some of the top-rated sites:

- The Quotations Page
- Famous Quotations Network
- Quoteland.com
- BrainyQuote

You can also get more specific in your online quote search, using keywords like "inspirational" or topic-specific keywords like "career quotes."

## Books

Although you'll certainly have no trouble finding quotes online, another great source of strong quotes is books. You can look for books of quotes and trade for them or buy them so you can cut them up, or you can borrow them from the library and copy the quotes that you like most.

Some popular books of quotations to consider include:

- *Quotable Quotes*
- *Great Quotes from Great Leaders*
- *Bartlett's Familiar Quotations*
- *The Book of Positive Quotations*

Don't limit yourself to just websites and books, though. Be on the lookout for sayings or phrases that speak to you. I came across one of my favorites in a page-a-day calendar several years ago.

## Adhesive

There are a number of ways to stick your photos, pieces of paper, and quotes onto the board, and each has advantages and disadvantages.

## Glue

The easiest and most common means of applying images to a board is glue. You dab some glue on either the board or the back of the photo or piece of paper and lay the item in place.

However, instead of using the gooier liquid glue, which can seep through the paper, opt for a glue stick to avoid damaging the ink. It's also harder to remove paper adhered with liquid glue than that adhered with a glue stick.

Acid-free glue is a good idea, especially if you're working with photos or images you can't replace. Acid-free or photo-safe glue won't damage photos like regular glue can.

Rubber cement is another option that has the same pros and cons as liquid glue. It's just smellier.

You can also use what scrapbook crafters use: Glue Dots. These little balls of glue are not wet, are easy to handle, and can be pushed into tight corners and will still stick, without being visible.

## Tape

If you're not sure which images you're going to feature on your vision board, or you want the ultimate flexibility to swap them out regularly, Scotch or masking tape is a good choice. It may tear the back of the paper when you remove it, but if you're careful, you'll probably be okay.

Double-sided tape is a good choice if you want something that will lie flat but not damage the ink or image, as wet glue can.

## Spray

Adhesive in a can, which frame makers use regularly to bind posters and art to foam core, is another great choice. It won't soak the paper you're gluing down, and items aren't usually stuck permanently. The only real downside is the difficulty in aiming the nozzle so as not to spray the entire board at once, so you may want to spray the back of the items you're gluing to the board, rather than the board itself. Since it's aerosol spray, be sure to work in a well-ventilated area.

## Photo Adhesives

A totally different approach is to use tiny frames or adhesive squares more commonly used with photos to mount items to the board.

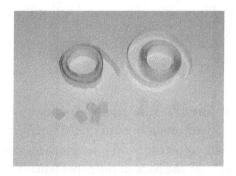

*You can use transparent photo squares to adhere a photo to a vision board without damaging it or them being seen, while photo corners add a little pizzazz and hold the photo in place*

To use these, you'll glue the tiny photo corners onto the board and place the square or rectangular images within them. It's a snazzy way to highlight your images while giving you the flexibility to change them, too. The only downside is that the images need to have ninety-degree-angle corners—they can be rectangular or square but not circular, or the corners won't be able to hold them.

You can also buy adhesive squares that go behind the photos and unobtrusively keep them stuck to the board.

## Pins

If you're using a corkboard or other bulletin board as your vision board, your best bet for holding your photos and phrases in place is tacks or pins, rather than glues or cements. So as not to obscure your photos, try to find pins with small heads–the round tops of larger tacks will cover portions of the images on your board.

# Display Options

After you've completed your vision board, you'll then need to decide how you're going to display it. It doesn't need to be available for all the world to see—some vision boards are very personal—but you should find a good way to keep your attention drawn to it. Generally, a frame provides both a way to contain the board and a way to hang it on a wall. However, if you plan to keep your vision board with you, such as in a notebook, you may want to laminate it to protect it, rather than adding a bulky frame.

## Traditional Frame

One option is to buy a plain traditional frame to showcase your board. Traditional frames are a good choice because they won't take away from the images featured on the board. Craft stores like Michael's, Hobby Lobby, and A.C. Moore carry large selections.

## Corkboard

On the other hand, if you're still figuring out what you want your future to be or have in it, a corkboard that allows you to easily add and remove images may be a good choice. You can find plain cork squares to apply to a wall or buy a framed corkboard that you can more easily hang and move around.

## Decorative Frame

Although the primary purpose of a frame is to allow you to hang your board, you can get creative with it, too. Buy an unfinished wooden frame and paint it yourself to showcase your vision board.

*Don't limit yourself to plain-jane frames. This artsy frame by Joanne Sharpe really dresses up a board and can draw your attention to your vision of your future.*

In the end, do whatever you can to help your vision board reflect you and what you're planning to do and have in your life.

## Summary

- Be clear up front about your vision for your future. That will make locating and selecting appropriate images much easier and will lead you to create a vision board that reinforces those goals, rather than confusing you.
- The type of backing you choose for your board, whether it's foam core, large-format paper, poster board, or cork, really doesn't matter. The most important consideration is whether it will allow you to fit all the images you desire and display the board prominently.
- You can find images in a wide variety of places, such as books, magazines, websites, travel brochures, college catalogs, and product-information materials, or by sifting through photos you have taken.
- To adhere the images and information to your board, use anything but liquid glue, which can seep through and damage the paper.

# CHAPTER 6

# What Your Board Should Look Like

Once you're armed with all your supplies, it's time to decide where exactly to place your pictures and inspiring phrases on your board. Although there are no hard-and-fast rules about what goes where on a board, you can take a few different approaches.

When you're finished, your vision board should be full of photos, images, illustrations, and words that represent the type of life you want for yourself. Keep in mind that it's a snapshot of what's important to you now, which could change as you achieve some of your goals. Be ready to reorient or replace images with ones that reflect new goals as you begin to make your vision a reality.

# A Vision Board's Role

Vision boards themselves help you conceive of and then more clearly envision your life as you want it to be. But simply slapping pictures on a board isn't enough—you need to understand the thinking behind why such boards work, and what you need to do to reap the rewards you're hoping for.

Karen Mann of Australia reports that she has made many vision boards over the past few years, manifesting many intentional, as well as some accidental, experiences. "There have been a number of times when something I have put on the vision board as a symbol for something I wanted has come true more literally than I intended at the time," she says. "One example was a Route 66 road sign, which I placed on my vision board to represent my dream of traveling in the U.S. However, not only did I get the opportunity to travel to the U.S., but I ended up driving along Route 66, entirely by accident. I was driving across country and took a wrong exit and found myself on a historic section of Route 66. It was a great detour that I enjoyed immensely."

## Clarity of Goals

An effective vision board features images and phrases that resonate with you—that excite and inspire you. The pictures and words don't have to be literal, such as showing the

Caribbean beach on which you want to sun yourself, but they should reflect where you're headed. If your goal is to retire in the Caribbean, you might have images of a more leisurely lifestyle alongside miles of pristine beaches. Otherwise, that beach image might propel you toward a short vacation there.

Or if you know you want to incorporate more volunteer work in your life, look for photos that depict that. For example, you may have an idea of a program you want to participate in, such as Rotary, or the type of action you'd like to take as an individual or as part of a group, such as rescuing abandoned dogs. Find images of the type of people, places, or things you want to support, and you'll draw to yourself the opportunities to work with them. But be as clear as possible about the relationship you want to have with this kind of work, or you may find yourself in a role you didn't exactly intend.

## Making a Dream Real

Research has shown that our brains will aid us in figuring out how to achieve the goals we set for ourselves, both consciously and subconsciously. For example, while you're awake and looking at your vision board, your brain may be actively problem solving, generating ideas for how to help you reach your goal. The same is true when you're asleep—your subconscious goes to work investigating various paths you could take to goal attainment.

In recent years, as mentioned in Chapter 2, the medical community has made some startling discoveries in the area of neuroplasticity. Although it was long assumed that the brain could not change or be changed, research on injured individuals has proven that assumption wrong. We can change the connections in our brain to enable new capabilities and compensate for others that may have been stunted. For example, people who go blind frequently find that their senses of smell and hearing become accentuated. And some stroke victims are able to regenerate synapses in their brains in new ways, to fully recover.

This is important for you because it means that you can retrain your brain. You can learn new skills and new habits and discover entirely new possibilities for yourself that you may never have thought possible.

## Your Most Important Goal

As you sort through the images and phrases you've gathered, look for the one that reflects your highest priority—your biggest goal. It might be the one that impacts all the rest, or simply what you're most interested in achieving. That might be as life-changing as moving cross-country to start a new career, finding the spouse you long for, or having a baby. Or maybe it's as concrete as obtaining the latest-model Lexus or having your child get all A's next semester.

Think of organizing your vision board as a process for sorting through what's most important to you—what will make you the happiest—rather than as a shopping trip through a department store. You'll have more success by thinking more broadly than about just a flat-screen TV or facelift as you evaluate where you want your life to head.

Place that top priority on your board first. By placing the image or phrase for your top priority first, you can then place the rest of your words and images around it. Don't glue anything down yet, because you want to be sure you have space for everything.

If the image that represents your top priority is on the small side, you could also take it to a copy shop and have it enlarged, to be sure it doesn't get lost among all the other images on your board.

Sometimes vision boards can become so cluttered with images and words that it's hard to see any individual item on there. To be sure that your biggest goals stand out, consider adhering them to larger pieces of contrasting colored paper to create paper frames or backdrops. This way, your most important images or phrases will stand out.

## Positioning

There are different schools of thought about image placement on a vision board, but the consensus seems to be that there is no wrong place to put your most important goal. Put it in the upper-right corner or lower-left corner, make it straight or crooked, enlarge it or keep it small—where it is located and its size won't impact your success.

However, some experts suggest not putting anything in the center. I'll tell you why in a minute, but you want to place your words and pictures around the outer edge of your board, without a clear center-oriented image.

## Sizing

Although there are no hard-and-fast guidelines regarding the minimum size of the photos you place in your board, you'll want to be sure any images related to your most important goal are clearly visible. Don't let them fade into the background by being too hard to see.

## What's in the Center

No matter what shape your board is—square, rectangular, triangular, or circular—you'll end up with a center point. You either can decide to place an image in the center, and I have a suggestion for what that photo should be of, or you can orient all your pictures and words so that nothing is in the direct center.

Erin Blaskie of Canada had always dreamed of owning an Audi TT Roadster. Yet when she came across a magazine photo of a BMW 128i convertible while preparing a vision board, something shifted in her. She tore it out and posted it on her board. Fast-forward six months to when Erin began test driving cars. The Audi didn't feel right; the BMW did. The only obstacle to her purchasing it was a large lump-sum payment. So close to having her car, Erin quickly created a new product she knew her customers wanted. When she made the product available for purchase on her company's website, she immediately generated, almost to the dollar, what she needed to buy her car. It now sits in her driveway.

### Nothing

Some students of the Law of Attraction argue that no image or words should be the central focus of the board. That's because whatever is in the center will become your primary focus, to the detriment of everything else on your board.

So if taking a trip to Tibet is one of your goals, and you place photos of Tibet in the center of your board, it's possible that you may manifest such a trip, but it may be at the expense of everything else on your board, such as family, health, finances, friends, and more.

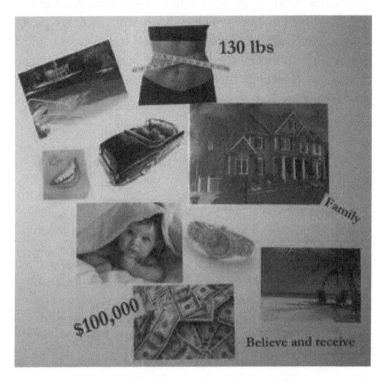

*No single image is the central focus of this board.*

A better approach would be to place your images off-center or in such a way that several overlap in the center, rather than having a single one dominate the center space—and your attention.

## Your Highest Priority

Although some vision board proponents recommend not centering images, others see no problem with it. Putting your biggest goal or priority in the middle of your board may cause you to think about it more than the others. However, this can be a positive rather than a negative, especially if that central goal is the catalyst for the rest of your goals.

For example, if you aim to significantly increase your income in the next few months in order to be able to afford a home, travel, a new car, or other lifestyle enhancements, it might make sense to put an image reflecting that in the center of your board, surrounded by the results of that income increase. Or if your biggest goal is to lose weight, you might put a photo of a slim body in the center, surrounded by images of all the things you'll be able to do when you have more energy and feel healthier, such as travel or embark on a career change.

*As the image of the baby has been placed in the center of this board, it is the most important image and goal.*

Whatever you focus on most is what your brain will devote the most resources to achieving.

Put soft, soothing instrumental or acoustic music on in the background as you begin to look for images and phrases that spark something in you or that represent your goals. The music will activate the part of your right brain that is responsible for creativity.

## You in the Center

An image in the center works well for some people, but you may find even greater success by putting *yourself* in the vision board—right smack dab in the center. Find a photo of yourself that you love, that shows you at your best, and place it in the center of your board. Then surround it with the people, places, things, and experiences you'd like to draw into your life.

When you see yourself at your best and link that image mentally with the other things on your vision board, you are training your brain to connect them—to see that those goals are possible.

*Seeing yourself surrounded by all that you want in your life can increase your confidence and your odds of success.*

This can be an effective approach if you find yourself feeling doubtful—doubting you can really achieve your goals or that you deserve them. When you see the picture of yourself you like most, you may feel more confident and self-assured. The feeling and belief that you can achieve your goals are critical to acquiring all that you place on your vision board.

## Order

As you begin to lay other images and phrases on your vision board, you may decide to lay them in an orderly fashion, carefully arranging them in an eye-pleasing manner first and then gluing them all later, or you may glue them down as you spot them in magazines.

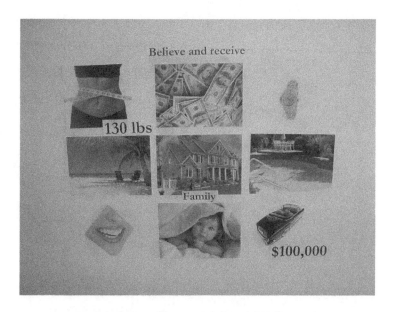

*A board with images and words placed in a neat and orderly fashion looks something like this.*

Being precise with your placement isn't required, especially if it interferes with your ability to view and imagine yourself having achieved each of the goals you've placed on the board. For some people, adding space between photos, overlapping them, or being less orderly can be more effective and more comfortable.

*There's nothing wrong with placing pictures more haphazardly—it may actually help you view the images from a different perspective.*

Many vision boards feature images and words that are placed randomly. When you approach the process as an artistic exercise, rather than a scientific or an academic one, you get a more free-flowing vision board. Each image is given equal weight. Some may have words or phrases pasted nearby, and others may stand alone. Some are big, some are little, some are covered by others—it doesn't really matter as long as you can still make out what each image is.

## Grouping

Another approach is to group like items together, such as family-related goals and dreams in one section of the board;

housing-related goals in another; and health, finance, and lifestyle dreams in other spaces on the board.

If this approach resonates with you, decide which section of your board will be devoted to each aspect of your life and then start sorting your images and phrases and placing them according to your categories. You can even add labels to the board to identify each category, if you like. This can be an especially good approach if you're working on achieving balance in your life.

Some feng shui practitioners who use vision boards, including Edward Mills (evolvingtimes.com), recommend that their students use the bagua map as a guide to organize images from the nine life areas.

## Prioritization

You can also choose to place the images and phrases you've gathered on the board in the order of importance to you, with the most important near the top or in a position of prominence, such as the center. The rest can be placed in relation to your top and most important goal, either fanning outward from the center or underneath it in a triangular shape.

One of the potential downsides of being so rigid in your prioritization is that you may be so focused on the goals that are most important to you that you overlook or miss other wonderful opportunities that come along in support of your other goals.

That's mainly because we have no control over when, where, or why God and the universe decide to present us with certain opportunities. We can't demand opportunities on our schedule, but rather must receive them when they are presented. That's the essence of why vision boards work—

they help us identify new opportunities that arrive in support of our dreams and aspirations.

> Jennifer Remling and her husband each had their own dreams. She wanted to write a book, and he wanted to buy an Airstream travel camper to be able to take weekend getaways. It suddenly dawned on Jennifer that they could do both—write the book *while* traveling around in the Airstream. So, she created a vision board with pictures from a brochure for a high-end, seventy thousand-dollar Airstream model and hung it in her office. Six months later, Airstream agreed to sponsor the couple's publishing efforts and gave them the exact model shown on Jennifer's vision board.

## To Frame or Not to Frame

After you create your vision board, whether it's the size of a large poster or small enough to fit in your wallet, you should consider how exactly you're going to display it. Or maybe you aren't. If you prefer to keep your goals private, you'll want to keep your board under wraps, maybe in a drawer, behind a filing cabinet, or in a room in your home others don't usually enter. If you want others to see where you're headed and what you're working toward, you may want to do more than simply tack your foam core to the wall.

### Frame Your Art

Since you've taken considerable time to select, place, and glue images you like to your board, why not put it under glass and frame it? This is an important piece in your collection, so why not treat it as such?

Local craft stores and even department stores have inexpensive frames of all shapes and sizes. You can choose a large poster-board frame with a thin layer of Plexiglas to contain your board, or a traditional or modern wooden or metal frame that really draws attention to your vision board. There is no wrong choice here; it's all a matter of preference.

Framing your vision board is likely to draw your attention to it more frequently, which is a plus, and you may feel more comfortable placing it in a position of prominence now that it's encased in an attractive frame.

## Staying Flexible

The only downside of framing your board, and perhaps the only reason not to, is that it will be harder to access it and move things around. And since the purpose of a vision board is to assist you in achieving your goals, you have to assume that, at some point, you'll need to get in there and update it by removing what you've obtained. You may also want to add a new goal you've set for yourself.

If you elect not to frame your board, some other options for displaying it include a mini easel, which you can place on top of a table or shelf to keep your vision board upright. You can also use Glue Dots as a temporary means of sticking your board to the wall without damaging either, as long as your board is fairly lightweight. The only thing you don't want to do is tuck your board away, out of sight, and then never pull it out again—that would be a reference board, not a vision board.

*A mini easel is a great way to display your
board without nailing it to the wall.*

## The Perfect Spot for It

Now that your vision board is ready to display, it's time to figure out where the heck to put it. It doesn't have to go on a wall, although hanging it on a wall does generally make it easier to see than if it gets caught up with clutter on a shelf or another spot.

### Make It the Focal Point

To get the best results from your vision board, it's important to make it the focal point of the room it is in. It doesn't matter which room—it could be a bedroom, kitchen, bathroom, office, or family room—but your eye should be drawn to it when you're there. You can also hang it outside your home—in your office, cubicle, or locker, for example.

> Mary Anne Brugnoni had been admiring the hand-crafted guitars designed by Steve Patience for six months but wasn't ready to make such a large investment. Nevertheless, she put a photo of several of his guitars on her vision board and spent a fair amount of time researching each one. Within a matter of months, following a series of emails with Patience, he offered her an amazing deal on the exact guitar she wanted.

Place it on the wall in such a way that it is easily visible from several places in the room, if you can. Don't hang it somewhere or put it on a shelf that can be seen only from the doorway, for example, or in a spot that is blocked by something else.

A better spot would be on a wall by itself. Even in a hallway is fine, especially if you pass by it regularly as you come and go.

## A Popular Spot

In addition to placing your board where you'll be able to see it, a smart choice, in terms of placement, is displaying it where you spend a lot of time. If you have a blank wall in your formal living room but you never go in there, it's a poor choice for your vision board. You need it to be where you will spy it routinely. Even in your garage on the wall in front of your car wouldn't be a bad idea, if you'd see it whenever you get in the car. Or in your laundry room, if you're the person who generally does all of the washing and drying.

## Summary

- Before you begin to glue images and words on your board, first plan where they will fit.
- Leaving space around each image will make it easier for your eyes to find them all and focus on them. A cluttered board would be overwhelming to your eyes and your brain.
- One approach to placing your images on your board is to leave nothing in the direct center. Put images down but try not to have one prominent image front and center, or else it will become a larger focus for you.
- Another approach is to put a photo of yourself that you love—one in which you look your best, perhaps showing you smiling and confident—in the center. Then surround yourself with what you desire in your life.
- You can also group related images on the board for easier focus and contemplation. If your brain likes to compartmentalize aspects of your life, this may be an effective way to place your images.

# CHAPTER 7

# The Catch-All Board

To keep track of all your to-dos and goals, you may create lists or use a fancy time-management system. Some of us separate our personal and work action items, and others lump them all together so as not to miss anything. The same options are available to you in creating a vision board or boards.

There is no right or wrong way to set up your vision board. Creating a catch-all board is simply one way of several to create and reflect on your life goals. You can identify the various aspects of your life that are important to you and create separate boards for each part of your life—one for relationships, one for finance, perhaps another for health. Or you can create one all-encompassing vision board—in terms of scope, not necessarily physical size—that reflects all the aspects of your life. This is a catch-all board—a central repository for goals in all the areas of your life.

## Why Centralizing Your Goals Is Cool

It can be overwhelming to think about the laundry list of things you need to do this week or this month. When you begin to review each and every "must-do" on your lengthy list, you may find your heart rate pick up a little.

Sure, you may blow off some of the less important—dare I say, "optional"?—commitments, but you're where you need to be most of the time. In addition, you address all the critical activities one way or another.

The same can be said for why all-encompassing vision boards work. They can be one spot where you place all your dreamed-of and hoped-for items. They are like your personal to-do list you carry with you. These life to-dos can include things like moving into the corner office you covet at work, obtaining the violin your daughter needs for her music aspirations, going on that spa weekend you'd love to take with the girls, or maybe even bringing home the puppy that's been appearing in your dreams recently.

You think about all your goals as parts of your life; one goal is not necessarily more important than another. Thinking about your goals as parts of artificial categories doesn't help you make progress on them, so you leave them on your master vision board, your catch-all.

## The Holistic Approach

Grouping career aspirations next to health goals, financial targets, and visions of your soul mate takes a *whole person,* or holistic, approach.

A whole-person view of life assumes that we are multifaceted, with the need to be fulfilled on many different fronts to feel happy. Focusing on only one or two aspects of life, such as money and career, typically leads to issues in other areas, such as relationships, spirituality, hobbies, and health.

If you rarely have the luxury of neatly compartmentalizing your life—your family intruding at work is the norm, and your fitness routine is frequently threatened by an overdue project at work, for example—an all-encompassing vision board is perhaps closest to what your everyday life is like. It's hectic.

Your life consists of overlapping responsibilities, priorities, and communications, as you juggle the many roles you fill—maybe daughter, son, sister, brother, employee, boss, teammate, student, wife, husband, volunteer, coach, teacher, mentor, leader, consumer. At any given moment, you're probably filling two or more of these roles at the same time. Together, they represent your life as a whole.

*This all-encompassing board shows goals*
*for many of life's facets and roles.*

This balancing act is exactly why a catch-all board works—it pulls together all your roles, responsibilities, hopes, and dreams in one place. Here, your brain can take it all in and work out exactly how you're going to make each and every one of your goals and dreams happen, without the need to refer to several separate boards.

Psychic messenger Terri Jay attributes her success with a vision board to her focus on the present, rather than wishing, hoping, and praying for the future. Already, she has manifested an F-350 Ford Crew Cab four-by-four truck, a new laptop, and her own show in Reno, Nevada. Her next goal? Her own national TV show, which she fully expects to realize. Terri says, "It's so important to focus on the feeling of what it is to have what you are trying to manifest. I actually sit in my desk chair and focus on my vision board and feel as if I am having my hair and make-up done for the TV show."

## Priorities Are Reinforced

Another advantage of producing a catch-all vision board is that it can help identify and reinforce your biggest priorities. The process of sorting and reflecting on the images you've gathered can help you clarify where you want to focus your attention.

As you examine each photo, illustration, drawing, or whatever you've collected, pay close attention to your gut reaction to it. What's your emotional response to the image and to the goal it represents? How strongly you react is a gauge of how connected you are to it—how big a priority it is for you. And you may find that, ultimately, some of the dreams you once had now aren't all that important.

For example, maybe you have always dreamed of hiking through Europe. You've talked about it forever and you get excited when you imagine what it would be like, but today when you look at all the other goals you now have for yourself, that trip may feel less important. That doesn't mean you should take the trip off your list of things to do in this lifetime, but if it's not a current goal, a current priority, don't put it on your vision board. What's on your vision board should represent goals and causes that you are passionate about and committed to achieving in the foreseeable future. Maybe that European trek is now more a wish than a burning desire.

## Your Intentions Committed to Paper

Because what you place on your board reflects what you're working toward, your board represents your current priorities. The words and images you've included aren't things you'd kind of like to have, or changes you'd maybe like to make someday. These are major experiences, things, relationships, or revelations you intend to bring into your life. They are what's important—your priorities.

### Your Subconscious Guide

The images of what you'd like to be, do, or have that are posted on your board are more than just pleasing pictures— they are also your brain's road map to success. As you choose pictures of what you want in your life, you are showing your conscious and subconscious mind what it should work toward helping you obtain.

Converting conscious thought into visual elements through the creation of a vision board activates the *reticular formation* in your brain. The reticular formation is a group of nerve endings located primarily in your brain stem that are responsible for, among other things, alertness and awareness. When you activate it, you make it almost hyperaware of your goals and dreams. This hyperawareness can help you spot opportunities you didn't notice before.

The strength of your connection to each picture—how you feel when you look at it—also helps your subconscious recognize how much energy to invest in accomplishing each goal. The more important each goal, the more your brain becomes aware of opportunities to get you on the path to achieving it. What you place on your board and focus on, imagining what it would feel like to have already obtained or achieved that goal, is what your brain then will show you how to accomplish.

## A More Balanced Life

Putting all your most important goals on one board also helps keep your life in balance, because you're including images from several aspects of your life. An all-encompassing board will likely have more than just career goals, or more than just relationship or health goals. By addressing the many facets of your life, an all-encompassing board helps you achieve a fulfilled and balanced life.

The beautiful poster of a silver-haired man and an attractive woman sitting on a dock overlooking turquoise water that Janet O'Connor spotted hanging in her local bank in Los Angeles captivated her so much that she requested one for herself. That image represented exactly the life Janet was after—the loving partner and idyllic locale.

So, she brought it home, mounted it, and hung on it on the back of her bedroom door, where she could look at it frequently. A year and a half later, Janet quit her job and moved, putting her in touch with a man very much like the one in the picture. They married and began looking for a home near the water. They can now sit on the beach together in Hawaii and look out over the turquoise ocean together, just like in the picture.

## Avoiding Intention Overload

Some people find that setting an intention is an important part of creating a vision board. To do that, you determine what the best possible outcome is and then decide that's what you will achieve. It's a mindset shift, focusing on the best-case scenario.

An intention is an objective, or a result. When you set an intention, you are mentally determining a planned result; you are focusing your mental energy on achieving a particular goal or end.

However, it takes energy to set an intention, to decide to focus on achieving your goals. And just as it takes more energy to complete twenty-five tasks than five, it's difficult for your brain to focus on and devote any significant energy to twenty-five items on your vision board. It makes more sense to choose only a few at most and set the intention to make real progress on those.

## Clutter Causes Confusion

Although an all-encompassing board makes a lot of sense, trying to include everything and the kitchen sink on one board can also be counterproductive. Yes, you may feel the need to address goals for every aspect of your life on your board, but if you have more than five to ten goals on there, you've also probably cluttered your vision board with intentions of little or no consequence.

Some goals that are appropriate for a catch-all board might include:

- Career objectives
- A financial or savings target
- Descriptions of a romantic partner
- Travel desires
- Philanthropic efforts
- Lifestyle changes
- Educational objectives
- Health improvements

There's a line between being thorough and being overloaded. If you cross it, your vision board will be cluttered and ineffective.

*A cluttered vision board is so busy that your
eyes can't find any one image to focus on.*

As with anything—your closet, your child's toy box, or your desk—the more you throw onto a surface, the more difficult it is for you to make out anything specific. Massive amounts of clutter, or data, are overwhelming, and your brain shuts down when faced with it. That's why it's important to feature only images of goals or intentions that are your highest priorities.

Sure, one of your life goals may be to win a Pulitzer Prize, but unless that's something you feel the need to make happen now, leave it off your vision board. Sometimes, less is more with respect to designing a vision board filled with goals you can work to achieve.

One thing to keep in mind is, when you apply images to your vision board, make sure they reflect what you truly want, and not what you *don't* want. Your brain can't differentiate between the two—it assumes what you're focusing on is what you want—which can backfire. So if you're trying to beat your personal best time in a triathlon, put the time you intend to achieve rather than crossing out your current personal best.

If you've whittled your selection of images down and it's still fairly large, you may want to try some graphic design tricks to make the most important intentions stand out. For example, you could make your most important goals larger in size or place them on top of a colored background to attract attention. Or you could overlay words and phrases atop your biggest goals and leave the smaller images blank or uncovered.

## Distraction Leads to Defeat

The biggest problem with clutter is that it's distracting. Your eyes don't know where to focus, and your brain can't take it all in. There's too much input at one time to sort through, so your brain doesn't. If your brain isn't on alert and looking out for opportunities to lead you to goal attainment, your odds of accomplishing your goals are virtually nil.

One way to tie all your goals and intentions together is to fill in any blank space behind the images and phrases you've placed on the board with color—cover up the remaining white space. This adds a sense of cohesiveness that enhances your ability to focus. Try painting or using Magic Markers or paper to cover any wide-open spaces in between pictures and words.

You are better off avoiding redundant images—photos or illustrations that are simply variations of one you already have on your vision board. If you've already featured a gorgeous new home on your board, you really don't need two or three or four more. Really, your brain gets it.

Likewise, scale back on the verbiage if you find your eyes can't focus on a particular saying or quote. The pictures are actually more important to the attraction process than the words, which are processed by your left brain—the logical side. Since your left brain isn't involved in awareness—that's all up to the right brain—peel off excess words to make the board less distracting.

## Summary

- Placing the images of all your goals and dreams on one vision board, instead of several separate boards, mirrors how you approach the many roles you currently fill.
- Investing creative energy in preparing a vision board activates the right side of your brain's reticular formation, which guides your awareness.
- The more aware your brain becomes of your goals and intentions, the more your conscious and subconscious minds work together to show you the paths to achieving them.
- Collecting in one place images to represent all of your current intentions is a more holistic approach, representing how intertwined your life roles and activities are.
- The only danger of creating a catch-all vision board is the tendency toward clutter—you may overdo it with images.

Want a little help figuring out what to put on your catch-all vision board? Use these questions to zero in on what makes sense for you and the life you envision.

What are the things in your life that bring you the most pleasure?

_____

_____

_____

_____

How do you currently spend your free time? What do you do?

_____

_____

_____

_____

How would you like to spend your free time if money were no object?

_____

_____

_____

_____

Are there any aspects of your life that you would change?

_____

_____

_____

_____

What would a dream day look like for you, if money were no object?

_____

_____

_____

_____

# PART 3

# Visions with a Purpose

When you understand the science behind vision boards and know how to apply images and words to your own, you can create several different types of vision boards.

You might choose a lifestyle board that encompasses many aspects of how you'd like your everyday life to be, or you might focus on an area of your life, such as your health, relationships, or finances. This part will help you craft the most effective board possible.

# PART 3

# Visions with a Purpose

# CHAPTER 8

# Your Best First Impression

Anyone who's ever gained a few extra pounds or been self-conscious about some aspect of his or her body (that's all of us, isn't it?!) may want to use a vision board to initiate some changes. Whether you're beginning a new phase of your life—maybe a new job, new relationship, or life in a new town—and want to make a great impression on people you meet, or you want to be more self-confident around folks you've known for years, you can enhance your image in plenty of ways.

Maybe you've always wanted to run the Boston Marathon, you'd like to trim ten pounds from your frame, or you think it would be great to ditch the glasses you've worn forever by having Lasik surgery. No one's saying you need to, but if these are personal goals you've set, a vision board can help you achieve success.

For any goal, it's important to ask yourself why you want to achieve it. Regarding your appearance, try to dig deep to determine why this goal is important to you. Are you trying to turn your health around and adopt healthier eating and living habits? Have you hit a plateau in your workouts, and you want to really make some progress? Have you been teased about some aspect of your appearance, such as your nose, your ears, or your belly?

Any reason you can come up with is reason enough to pursue your goals, but just be clear and upfront about why you want to, so that you're realistic about any reaction you may get from others.

## A Weight Change

With all the current attention on obesity, it's hard not to be self-conscious about weight, no matter what your weight may be. And while most of us would rather be slimmer than we are, it can be difficult to curb the expansion in our middles. Fortunately, a vision board can be the push you need to start making changes that generate results.

## Your Goal Weight

It all starts by deciding on your goal weight. What number are you aiming for to look your best? What would you look like at that weight? Do you have photos when you were that weight in the past? If so, pull them out and place them on your vision board. Seeing that you were once at your goal weight will reinforce that you can do it—because you've already been there. Or if you've never been at your goal weight, look for images of people at your desired weight and replace their head with yours. That way, when you see the image you'll begin to imagine yourself at that weight.

Also look for photos of people who appear to be the weight that you want to be and use those, maybe in the background of your board.

## Write It Down

Next, and this is important, write your target number down or type it up on the computer, print it out, and put it on your vision board. Remind yourself of what number you want to see on the scale.

## Your Plan

Now that you've imagined what you'll look like at your target weight and you've committed to reaching it, it's time to get specific about how you'll get there. Looking at your vision board will energize you and remind you of your intention, but unless you march in place or walk on a treadmill as you look at your vision board (which is a darn good idea, come to think of it), you won't burn enough calories to make much headway.

Some other images to consider posting on your board are pictures of people exercising in ways that interest you. Do you like walking? Look for pictures of walkers. Do you like to work out in a gym? If so, gym pictures shouldn't be hard to find—just do an online search for a major gym chain and print out photos of people exercising there (keeping in mind that this is okay only if it's for your personal use, due to copyright laws).

*Incorporate images and words that remind*
*you of the weight-loss path you're on.*

## Acting as If

Another tool in the world of visualization is focusing on the feeling of having reached your goal. When you look at the photos of you at your desired weight, really imagine and try to feel what being at that weight will be like. Doing this will stimulate and help train your brain to keep you on course.

Indi Avila had always struggled with her weight, but when she gained fifty-five pounds during her pregnancy, she knew it was time to get serious. So she created a cork vision board. On her board she wrote, "I promise to be lean for life so that..." and then she outlined five reasons losing weight was important to her. On the bottom she wrote in large letters: "My current goal weight is 112 lbs." Finally, she joined a weight-loss program and watched the pounds melt off. Having the *what*—weight loss—and the *why*—her five reasons—on her board to look at constantly "was a huge aid," she says.

## Your Body

Although weight loss is a goal for many Americans, perhaps you're more focused on how your body performs—what it's capable of—than on what the scale reads. If so, you'll be on the hunt for images and words that reinforce your physical abilities. That could include stamina (such as being able to keep up with your young children), weight-lifting strength, speed, or your performance in a competition.

## Appearance

To set goals for your body's appearance on your vision board, look for pictures of men or women who resemble you and who have the body shape you're after. Maybe you want a more toned physique or more muscular arms or legs. Whatever shape you're after, keep an eye out for those types of photos. Magazines dedicated to health and fitness are excellent sources of such images. You can also flip through stock images to find, for example, athletes in action.

## Muscles

If your particular interest is in developing larger muscles, flipping through bodybuilding magazines and websites should provide plenty of pictures to place on your board. Brochures from bodybuilding-oriented gyms are another potential source of vision board materials. Words to accompany the photos might include your current weight-lifting goals, a regimen you want to adhere to, or a particular event you want to win.

## Performance

You may also be in a crowd that pays less attention to how big your butt is and more to whether you can run a five-minute mile. If so, your vision board images should show people pushing their bodies to the limit.

If you're a bicyclist, make sure you feature other top-performing bicyclists. If you're a runner, there should be pictures of runners on your board—even better if there's one of you crossing the finish line. Whatever your sport of choice—

rowing, rugby, baseball, swimming, or tennis, to name a few—incorporate images of people participating in it and match the images with words and phrases that set new goals for yourself.

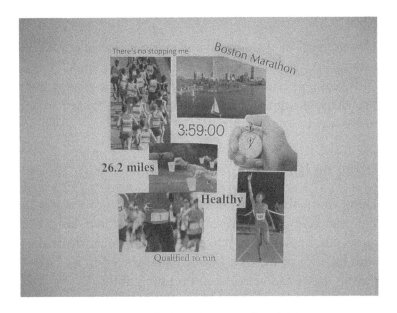

*Feature images that show toned and fit people doing what you aspire to physically.*

## How You'll Achieve Your Goal

As with anything, in addition to gluing aspirational and inspirational photos to your board, start to ponder how you'll make the leaps in performance you want. What aspect of your training can you change? Maybe you really need different equipment or a new coach for some aspect of your game. After you've identified some specific areas you can work on, add images of those to your board. Seeing them regularly on your board will remind you of the steps you're taking to improve.

# Your Hairstyle

One of the most obvious and noticeable aspects of our bodies is our hair. Is it long, short, thin, thick, brown, blond, black, curly, straight, brushed, or braided? There are myriad options that shape our appearance, and changing your hairstyle is one major way to impact your look.

## Choosing Your Look

Using your vision board to select and commit to a new hairstyle can be exciting and scary at the same time. Sure, hair grows out, but it can seem to take forever if you're dissatisfied with the cut you just got. Maybe that's where you are now—getting over a bad haircut and dreaming of the day you'll be able to look more attractive.

If that's the case, it's time to pull out consumer magazines, especially hairstyle publications, and hunt for the perfect haircut for your face. Rather than studying the images intently, flip casually through the magazines and see what style instinctively catches your eye—that's a better gauge of what appeals to you.

Manifestation

Want to see what you'd look like in a variety of styles and colors before committing to anything? Check out InStyle's Hair Try-On app. It's a free service that lets you upload an image of yourself and then virtually try on different styles. When you find one you like, print it out and post it on your vision board.

## How You'll Feel

Your appearance shapes so much of your personality and self-confidence that it's especially important to imagine what you'll feel like as the new and improved you. Are you more feminine? More handsome? More confident? Sexy? Outgoing? Picture yourself with your new hairstyle and notice the internal changes that occur.

## Skin

Another part of our anatomy that draws scrutiny is our skin. Is it healthy, glowing, and smooth, or pale and marked with blemishes or scars? Your skin is one part of your body that's out there for everyone to see. You can put a hat on your head and dress in oversized, formless clothing to cover a few extra pounds, but unless you're Michael Jackson, you probably don't generally wear a mask to hide your face.

If your skin is one area where you'd really like to see changes, you'll want to be sure it's on your vision board.

## The Changes You'd Like to Make

Flipping through fashion or women's magazines should provide you ample examples of flawless-looking skin (you know they've been airbrushed, right?) to paste onto your board. If there are certain areas of your face that you feel need some attention, cut out images of those sections in addition to full-face images. You may even want to do a before-and-after series showing your face now and after you've made some changes.

## What You're Going to Do About It

There are a number of approaches you can take to improving your skin's appearance and skin tone. One might be to change your diet and skincare routines; you can place the new ones on your board to remind you. Another might be to see a dermatologist for some recommendations. You could also make an appointment to see an aesthetician or the professional behind your favorite make-up brand's counter. Then again, maybe it's time to check out a new make-up line if you're not satisfied with your current appearance.

You have many options, so take some time to clear your mind and let the right path come to you. Then place images of it on your board to get you going toward achieving your vision of yourself.

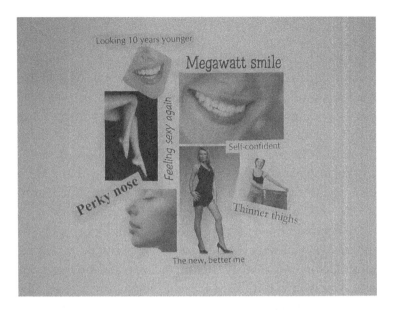

*For an appearance-focused vision board, track down images showing the hair, skin, and teeth you'd rather have.*

## Your Smile

Over the past decade, straight, gleaming white teeth have become the new standard. The whiter and prettier your teeth, the more attractive you're perceived to be, at least according to Hollywood. This is why so many cosmetic dentists now exist, offering tooth whitening and straightening without metal braces.

There is nothing wrong with desiring white, straight teeth, of course, and if that's on your list of priorities, your vision board can show you how to attain it.

## Changes to Your Teeth

Start by describing what you want your smile to look like and how that's different from what you have now. Maybe you need a gap filled in between two teeth, or maybe you have some overlapping that needs to be relieved. If you have any missing or discolored teeth, many procedures can fill them in, get rid of stains, or cover any broken or chipped teeth.

Begin by stating what it is you want changed and then looking for images of the smile you want to have. Here, too, a before-and-after of your smile can be very motivating.

Sometimes finances appear to be a roadblock to some of the changes you want to make to your appearance. However, most doctors and dentists offer financing plans and may even negotiate with you, to help get you the assistance you want. If money is an issue, put that on your board, too, so you can move forward with your goals.

## Getting That Perfect Smile

Your next step is to carefully study your vision board and determine what it is you need to do to make progress toward your goals. Maybe you need to make an appointment with a dentist who specializes in your issues, whether that's an orthodontist, an endodontist, or a cosmetic dentist. Or, even before that, research who's the best candidate to help you. You may not even be aware of what's possible yet, but gathering images and posting them on your vision board is a great start.

## Summary

- Since your outward appearance shapes the impression people have of you, reflect on what aspects of your appearance you're self-conscious about.
- Images to support a new weight-loss program should be positive and reflect the slimmer, healthier you you're working toward. Including pictures of how you'll achieve that reduction—such as a workout routine at a gym, a new running habit, or a diet plan—will reinforce your conscious acts.
- If your goal to become healthy has more to do with physical performance and overall muscle tone, rather than vanity, the images on your vision board may include performance targets, such as times, weights, or distances.
- Images of desired physical changes, such as a new hairstyle; whiter, straighter teeth; or smoother, more taught skin, can help you decide how to proceed in bringing about these changes.

Want a little help figuring out what to put on your first-impression vision board? Use these questions to zero in on your desired appearance.

How would you describe yourself physically right now?

_____

_____

_____

_____

What changes would you make to your physical appearance if you could?

_____

_____

_____

_____

What do you consider to be your best features?

_____

_____

_____

_____

What features would you like to change if you could?

_____

_____

_____

_____

Are there any goals you'd like to set for yourself in terms of physical performance, such as running, lifting weights, climbing, or engaging in some other sport?

_____

_____

_____

_____

Do you have any sports role models?

_____

_____

_____

_____

## CHAPTER 9

# Designing Your Dream Career

Vision boards can be used to manifest everything from tangible things, such as products, to intangible things, such as experiences and new career opportunities. A vision board created to support your career goals might include images of the organization you want to work for, the type of job you want to hold, or the roles and responsibilities you aim to have in your dream position.

Before you can start visualizing and envisioning your new career, you'll want to be clear about exactly what it looks and feels like. In your dream role, what are you doing, who are you working for, what kinds of challenges do you face, and where are you based? If you haven't already articulated the answers to those questions, take a step back and imagine the perfect workday. Then create a vision board to make that a reality.

## What Kind of Job Do You Want?

One of the best ways to start imagining your dream career is to think about what you love to do. That may be what you currently do to earn a living, something you do as a hobby or pastime, or something you've always wanted to try. Past experience has little to do with your success in attracting your dream job, because you can uncover opportunities that will get you the experience you need and lead to your ultimate position.

### Industry-Specific Aspirations

Is there a particular field or industry you've always wanted to work in or that you'd like to get back into? Just because you currently work on Wall Street doesn't mean you can't move into the beauty industry, or vice versa. Or if you're finding that your current job in accounting just isn't cutting it and you want to move into teaching, there's no reason you can't. Perhaps you spend all your waking hours playing video games but have never considered that you could make a career out of it—now is the time to rethink that.

What field or vocation intrigues you? What industry has always held your interest? When you have a sense of the industry you want to play a role in, it's time to look for images to place on your board.

The best places to find industry or vocational images are trade journals—magazines devoted to covering a particular type of business or industry. These are different from general business magazines such as *Businessweek* or *Forbes,* for example, and include titles such as *Chemical Week* and *Sporting Goods Business.*

As you peruse your target industry's magazines, you should be able to find a wide variety of images and phrases that will work perfectly on your vision board. In addition to photos of people in action, look for images of workplaces, successful projects, best practices, and help wanted ads that closely match your desired job. Be sure to keep an eye out for words and phrases that are common in the industry.

Odds are good that there is a magazine out there for the industry you want to be part of. WebWire has its own trade magazine directory you can search: webwire.com/IndustryList.asp.

Although it is not all-inclusive, it's a good place to start.

## A New Role

You can also create a vision board to help you pursue a different role within your current industry or company, such as a promotion or a transfer into a new area.

To reflect that change on your vision board, you might feature images of people wearing clothes appropriate for your desired position.

For example, if you're a medical student with eyes on the chief resident role, you might find a picture of a lab coat with "Chief Resident" embroidered on it. Or if you're an attorney hoping to be given partner status soon, you might collect photos from fashion magazines of more upscale outfits a partner would wear. Whatever outward appearance that indicates the new role—clothing, a special ID tag, a business card, a résumé, and the like—those are the types of images you should look for or create yourself.

Don't limit yourself only to magazines for your image search. You may find it easier to create a new business card using an online service like Vistaprint, for example, and then print out the sample you create on-screen to adhere to your board; let your employer spring for the actual cards after you're given the new position. You could also take photos of yourself trying on a beautiful custom suit at a local boutique and have them printed. In fact, the more you are present (via photos) in the images on the board, the more confident you'll grow about your goals and dreams.

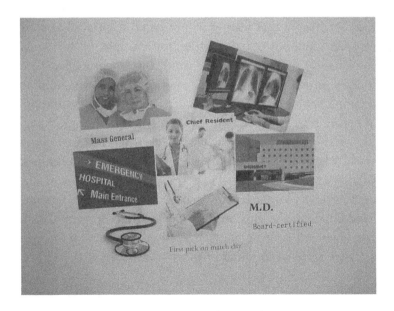

*A vision board devoted to a job promotion might look something like this.*

# Your Ideal Employer

Your career goals may also be focused on working for a particular company or organization. Maybe you've always wanted to work for Apple, or it's been your dream to be a Disney employee. Perhaps your goals aren't as specific—you just know you'd be happier working in a day care center, at an advertising agency, or as a software developer.

## The One and Only Organization

If there is a particular organization that you admire and would like to be employed by, then your vision board images should be focused on the company, its location, and its products. If there is a particular division you want to work in, look for images that feature its products, awards it has won, or other mentions of its activities, for example.

In addition to looking at your vision board filled with images related to your dream employer, you also need to imagine how it will feel to be a part of that organization. Whether it's a construction firm, cruise line, or bank, imagine what your day is like, what you do when you first get to work, what you wear, and how you feel. Really get a sense of what your new job will feel like. Imagine how proud you'll be to announce to your friends that you now work for Google, Madonna, or the Boston Red Sox—whoever your dream employer is. Picturing yourself as an employee is an important part of the vision board process—don't skip it.

A few years ago, Jessica Fletcher was finishing school in Minneapolis and dreaming of a life in New York City as a stand-up comedian. To stay motivated, she drew a giant picture of New York City and hung it on her wall by the front door so she'd see it every time she entered the apartment. To prepare for her move, she began going to open-mike nights in Minneapolis, practicing her stand-up routines, and scanning Craigslist for jobs and apartments in New York. Just four months later, she made the move, and now she performs in clubs around the city, such as the Broadway Comedy Club and the Gotham Comedy Club.

## A Type of Firm

If you haven't zeroed in on one potential employer, don't worry. That's fine! That means you're open to a wider range of future employment opportunities, which may open doors you hadn't even conceived of.

Sometimes it can be helpful to seek out a career counselor if you feel you need guidance in the types of work settings that would best fit your ambitions and personality. There are also plenty of career tests and assessments that can guide you to your perfect match.

In order to create a career-focused vision board, it's helpful to have some sense of where you will best fit. Maybe you know that you want to work in Miami, be part of a fast-paced real estate office, or join a laid-back veterinary clinic. The more clearly you can picture the type of business you want to work for, the easier it will be to attract that opportunity. The more vague, the more varied your options—which isn't necessarily a bad thing. However, it may take you longer to find your best work situation if you aren't sure what you want.

## Higher Salary

For many workers, the most important measure of success is how large their paycheck is—how much money the job pays. If you're happy with where you work and what you do but you'd really love to make more money at it, your vision board should be very financially oriented.

### The Size of Your Paycheck

The easiest way to visualize more money coming in from your job is through your weekly, biweekly, or monthly paycheck. How large would you like that check to be? Visualize the amount and then create one for your vision board. One way to do that is to photocopy a recent paycheck—don't use the actual check—white-out the amount, and write in the amount you want to see in the future. Get used to seeing that amount on the dotted line. Think about what it would feel like to have access to that amount of money each pay period.

Consider what it would take for you to make that leap. Would you need to be promoted in order to move into a different salary bracket? Would you need to have one or more exemplary performance reviews? Or would you need to demonstrate your worth to the company, perhaps by landing a major account or finding a way to significantly improve some aspect of its operations?

Many organizations today have programs to reward employees for certain behaviors. Some companies pay employees who suggest improvements to work processes, giving them a percentage of the money earned or saved. Other organizations reward workers who recruit other workers—sometimes quite handsomely! In addition to working on boosting your paycheck, look for other programs and offerings that can help you demonstrate your value to your employer.

Now that you know what number you're seeking, put it on your vision board, along with any other changes you imagine would come with it. Would you receive a promotion? Earn that coveted corner office? Be assigned a team to supervise? Also include images of how your life would change with that additional cash. Would you be able to buy a bigger house, get a new car, or join the local country club? What will that money do for you?

## The Size of Your Annual Increase

Some people evaluate their performance more on the size of their raise than on the actual dollar value. This is especially relevant in firms that express financials in percentages rather than actual dollars.

If you work for an organization that looks at the world in terms of percentages, you'll want your vision board to be in sync. You may want to try to get a copy of the measuring device your company uses to determine how much of an increase people receive, based on their performance. You can then mark where you aim to be. Or type the percent increase you expect in large numbers and put it on your board. Include other photos that represent what you're willing to do to demonstrate you're worthy of that big bump. For example, will you volunteer to take over a failing project or a task no one else wants? Will you start arriving early and working late? Or maybe you'll apply to go back to school to get some extra training your boss has been hinting would be a smart career move.

## Receiving Recognition

For some people, money isn't as big a motivator as recognition of their fine work. If you fall into this camp, you'll want to think about what kind of recognition would mean the most to you. Do you revel in public praise, maybe in front of a large audience? Does the person giving the praise mean more than the number of people who hear it? Do you want to be recognized for something in particular, such as being credited with an important find or successful project?

### An Impressive Title

Your goal may be to attain a specific job title to reflect your accomplishments or level of skill or seniority in your job. If that sounds like you, you'll want to include on your vision board both the title you want and any ancillary benefits, such as new letterhead, a new uniform, or some other outward distinction. Find pictures of the other ways that title will be evident to all and include them on your board.

The movie *Rudy*, about Daniel "Rudy" Ruettiger, reflects the single-mindedness of purpose that yields career success. Rudy was a high school football player whose lifelong dream was to play for the University of Notre Dame. When he failed to be admitted to his dream school, he enrolled at a junior college, determined to transfer to Notre Dame. He did, finally, during his last semester of eligibility, and tried out for the football team. He made only the practice team, but because of his spirit and persistence he was given the chance to play on the varsity team during the last game of the season.

## An Award for Your Performance

Sometimes even more than a title, which can be changed or taken away, an official award or honor is more prized. Is there a regular honor bestowed on an individual you'd like to receive? Many companies have an "employee of the month," for example. Or is there a major award given only to the most deserving individual, for some behavior or performance?

Whatever the honor, find pictures of what you would receive when you win the award and place those on your board. Maybe it's a plaque, a banner strung across the front of the corporate headquarters, or a press release sent out to the national media touting your accomplishments. Identify all the aspects of the recognition you desire and piece them together on your board.

*If you're pursuing career recognition and reward more than change, your vision board might look something like this.*

## Additional Perks

Maybe there's nothing wrong with your job or career—you may even love it just as it is—but you may still desire more confirmation of your worth to your organization. You may want some outward signs of your value. Typically, those signs come in the form of money, such as a performance incentive or salary increase. Or perhaps control over your own private slush, I mean expense, fund.

## Bonuses

Another possible monetary reward is a performance bonus if you've been exceeding your performance targets in your current job. Typically, these would occur following a salary review, but you can request an interim performance appraisal if you feel you deserve some special consideration.

Or if you're feeling underappreciated at your current job, you could explore opportunities elsewhere, where you may be able to negotiate a signing bonus for making a switch. Although they are rarer today than even just a few years ago, signing bonuses are a measure of how much a particular employer wants you. In the 1980s, major consulting firms were rumored to pay newly-minted MBAs from top schools thirty thousand dollars or more just to commit to working there. That money was in addition to the sizable salary.

If you're considering a job or career change and know that a signing bonus is a possibility—in some industries it's unheard of—decide what amount you want. Then print out a picture of that amount in dollar bills, create a check for the amount, or print out the amount from your computer and post it on your vision board.

## Company Car

Another desirable bonus for working at some organizations is a company car. Sometimes companies assign cars based on the fleet they already own, and others give employees a car allowance and permit the employee to decide how to spend it. Some people who get these apply the allowance toward a luxury car, and others prefer not to take on an auto loan beyond the value of their allowance.

If your goal is a company car, think about exactly what kind of car you would get. Do you care? For many people, access to an additional car—whatever the make and model—is a reason to smile. On your board, show what kind of car you'll be driving, maybe how much it will ultimately cost you beyond the allowance provided, and imagine how great you'll feel to be driving it.

## Expense Allowance

Maybe a car isn't your big desire, but control over your own expense account is. Maybe being able to wine and dine clients and suppliers whenever you like or take care of purchases for use at the office without whipping out your own personal credit card to be reimbursed later is your idea of a step up.

If it is, find images of how you would tap into that expense account. Would you be given a corporate credit card? Are there restrictions on what that money can be used for? What are the ways that you'll spend it? Put that all on your board.

## Access to Training

Employees with ambition often recognize the value of additional training and professional development. Even more than cash, the opportunity to receive skills training or to enroll in a certificate- or degree-granting program can be life-changing.

If your vision for your future includes additional schooling or participation in a specific training program, mentoring group, or mastermind group, identify it by name and feature it on your vision board. A mastermind group consists of several people committed to sharing what they know and helping each other improve and succeed. Typically consisting of fewer than twenty participants, members of mastermind groups help each other solve problems, and they brainstorm solutions, give feedback and share resources to aid and support one another.

## Summary

- You might create a career vision board to help you make a major move or to enhance the job you currently have. Or maybe you love your job, but you'd like to enjoy a more comfortable lifestyle.
- If you have always wanted to work for a particular company or organization, gather images and words that are all about that business.
- Think about what motivates you—money, recognition, or perks, for example—and include images on your board that will bring you more of what you want.
- In many cases, superior performance is required to qualify for major bonuses, salary increases, or reward programs, so consider looking for pictures of people doing what you know you'll need to do to attain your goals.

Want a little help figuring out what to put on your dream career vision board? Use these questions to zero in on what your perfect job looks like.

What would your dream job look like? What would you do on a daily basis?

_____

_____

_____

_____

What types of tasks are easy for you?

_____

_____

_____

_____

What kind of training, if any, would you need to qualify for your dream job?

_____

_____

_____

_____

What companies do you aspire to work for?

_____

_____

_____

_____

What is it about those companies that is appealing to you?

_____

_____

_____

_____

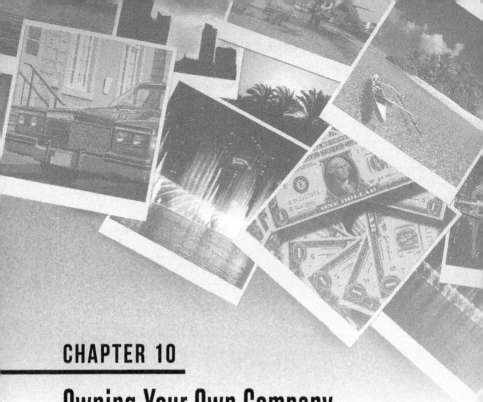

# CHAPTER 10

# Owning Your Own Company

The dream of owning a business is familiar to many. If it's also your dream, your vision board can help you zero in on exactly what your business will do, what it will sell, and how you can apply your innate skills and interests to make it successful.

To start your board, think through what kind of company best fits your interests, abilities, and experience. Then you can consider the types of customers you want to serve and what your company will look like as it becomes more and more visible and successful.

# You, Inc.

Because your business is a reflection of you, including your background, experience, interests, personality, and work style, it's important for your vision board to match the type of venture you envision. If you include vague photos and unclear concepts of what your business will offer your customers, you could end up with exactly that—an amorphous business with an unclear product offering. That's not how companies become successful.

## Your Industry

Before you even start looking for images and phrases that illustrate the type of company you want to own, think about what industry you want to be in. Are you a retailer by heart or a chef? Are you drawn more to technology and software development or to art and creative pursuits? Do you love working with your hands, maybe as a welder or an auto technician?

*If owning your own business is a dream you're trying to manifest, you'll want to create a board like this.*

If you're not sure about your preferences, consider what industry your parents were in. Sometimes that's a useful starting point, because you may be familiar with their line of work. Or have you had jobs during your career that you enjoyed more than others? Past experience can be extremely useful in getting up and running quickly and in avoiding common pitfalls in certain kinds of businesses, but if you're not passionate about the types of organizations you've worked in before, don't feel compelled to continue in those fields.

Jen Smith, "The Millionaire Mommy Next Door," created her first vision board, which she calls "a treasure map to a rich life," in her early twenties. Back then, she was earning minimum wage, one paycheck away from homelessness. Creating a vision board helped Jen define the life she wanted and reminded her of her dreams and aspirations. By age forty, she was living her vision—she and her husband had become successful, happy, debt-free millionaires. Now, every few years, as life experiences modify some aspect of her aspirations and passions, she designs a new treasure map. "Lo and behold, my life soon morphs to fit my new vision," she says. "And it repeats over and over again."

If you can identify an industry you're interested in and the type of work you'd like to do as a business owner, it's time to start looking for images that reflect your new role as an entrepreneur. General business magazines, such as *Fortune, Entrepreneur, Black Enterprise,* and *Businessweek,* are excellent sources of entrepreneurial images. Trade journals specific to your industry are even better, because they contain photos of people on the job and in a work setting that may be similar to what you picture for yourself.

Another great source of photos is brochures from companies in your desired industry. Simply call and ask for an information packet to be sent to you; stating that you intend to start a competing company may not be the best approach, however. It's better to be vague. Industry, trade, or local merchant associations, too, have imagery that they may be willing to share with you. Start by requesting membership information, which should at least net you a color brochure.

Look for or draw pictures of the many different aspects of your business so you can more completely imagine it. What does the building look like? Do you have many employees or just a few? Do you have a warehouse? Who are your customers? The more steps in the business process you show, the clearer your path to success will be.

## What You Sell

After picturing the industry you want to work in, it's time to decide what you'll sell. The two biggest choices are products and services. You can sell products by themselves, like edible fruit bouquets or clothing, or you can sell services, such as consulting or hairstyling. You can also sell both, such as auto dealerships that sell cars and repair them under the same roof.

Products are a tangible and deliverable, while services are frequently intangible.

Tangible goods can be touched and held; they have mass. Intangible things do not have mass. Tangible items are things such as food, furniture, and pets. Intangibles are services such as cleaning, computer repair, and home security. You can't necessarily see or touch the process, but you can see the result of the work done.

Your vision board should show exactly what you'll be selling customers, whether it's products or services, as well as anything that makes what you'll be selling particularly special.

## Customers Served

Picturing who your customers are can be challenging and rewarding at the same time—because the more specific you are about who you want to work with, the likelier your vision board can help attract those exact buyers to your business. Believing that "everyone" is your customer and showing random people on your vision board is dangerous. In truth, everyone is not your customer, nor do you really want to do business with everyone; there are good customers and there are bad customers, and you need a filter to try to weed out those who aren't a good fit.

One filter could be how much money you expect your customers to spend with you per transaction, per project, or per month. That will eliminate some prospects right off the bat. Another filter might be whether the customers are individuals or organizations. In fact, that's an important distinction you'll want to make upfront.

### Business-to-Business

When your business sells to other businesses, you are deemed a business-to-business (B2B) venture. Examples are marketing consultants who sell to telecommunications companies, banks that serve small businesses, sign businesses that create directional signs for organizations, and event planners who manage trade shows.

A technique some of the best salespeople use that you should, too, is to make a list of your top prospects by name.

This helps you remain clear about who your target customers are. Post that list on your vision board. Seeing those company names day after day will make you more aware of networking and business opportunities and ultimately help you earn their business.

Images of your corporate customers could include photos of large office buildings; photos inside a boardroom, where someone like you might be making a presentation; photos of someone providing the services you offer in a corporate environment; or photos of the logos of the companies you most want to do business with.

## Business-to-Consumer

If your business is dedicated to helping individuals, you run a business-to-consumer (B2C) company. Instead of focusing your sales process on getting your foot in the door at an organization, you're trying to attract individual customers. Examples of B2C businesses include house-cleaning services, restaurants, home builders, attorneys who deal in personal matters, and retail shoe stores.

Images of your customers on your vision board would show more person-to-person contact, more individuals, and perhaps some images of where you'll be providing your products or services—in a mall, at someone's home, or in a store, for example. Find images that reflect what your perfect day will look like as a business owner, and feature those to help you truly feel what it will be like to run your own show.

# Financial Rewards

One of the biggest reasons people start their own businesses is the potential financial reward that can result. 84 percent of

American millionaires work for themselves; only 16 percent of them work for someone else. If you're among the many who enjoy being paid for their performance, running your own business can be lucrative—especially when you envision it clearly and follow that path.

## It's All About the Money

Because you're clear about your business's mission, customers, and specialness, you're able to shape it into a highly successful venture. In most cases, being successful means that you have plenty of customers who appreciate what you sell them, buy from you frequently, and pay enough that you earn a profit on each transaction. With that foundation and as your business expands through a widening net of satisfied customers, you earn more and more money. As long as you invest a portion of it back in the business, you can create an ongoing, sustainable source of revenue.

On your vision board, you might reflect your business's success in pictures of scads of customers, long lines out the door of your business, an overflowing cash flow, piles of money, and a real-looking bank statement with millions of dollars.

Putting pictures of money on your board is fine as long as there is some connection to what the money will do for you—how you will spend it. Asking for loads of money is too vague a request. Think about the *why*. Be as specific as possible, such as, "I want to make twenty thousand dollars in the next three months to be able to totally redesign the corporate website."

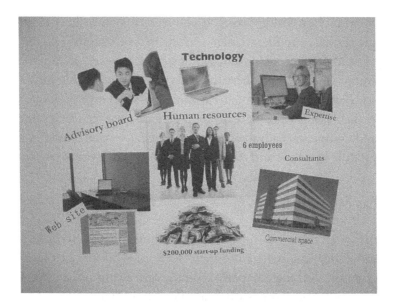

*If you need specific resources to make your business
a go, create a board devoted to attracting them.*

## Property, Plant, and Equipment

Another potential benefit of starting and running your own
business is that you can invest in other revenue-producing
instruments. No, I'm not talking trumpets and violins but
rather real estate and big machinery. As your venture brings
in more dough, you can diversify and buy other things that
will generate more money or appreciate in value.

One such instrument is real estate. Maybe you can fore-
see buying a building to house your company or investing in
commercial or rental property separate from the business. If
so, find pictures of similar properties or maybe even properties
that are currently on the market that you'd like to own. Add

them to your vision board. If you have a goal for how many properties you'd like to own, include that on your board, too.

Other revenue-producing instruments are production equipment and machinery that give you an edge in your industry. Being the only company within a hundred miles that has a particular high-end piece of equipment can be a source of pride and competitive advantage. If that's a goal of yours, request a product brochure and paste photos of it on your vision board.

## Your Home Away from Home

Although money is the most obvious outward sign of success, some business owners use their office or workspace to indicate how well the company is doing. Since your office, storefront, or warehouse is often a reflection of your personality, imagine how you'll decorate it. The images on your vision board should match that.

### Location, Location, Location

First, visualize where your business will be located. Are you setting up a home-based operation, or do you want to have a separate space to head to in the morning? If so, how far away do you want it to be? Does it need to be where all the action is, maybe downtown, or is a suburban luxury space more in keeping with the company's style and image?

Flip through local newspapers and magazines to find photos of local office parks, buildings, or neighborhoods in which you want to locate your business. You can also print out a map from MapQuest and put thumbtacks on streets or corners where you'd like to find a space.

Call your local Convention and Visitors Bureau for photos of your surrounding area. These agencies almost always have shots of skylines and major buildings available, often at no charge. Scour those for any featuring the building you intend to work in. Another good source is Zillow, which has individual property information.

## Style

You may want to focus on how you'll decorate your workspace while you manifest your own building. Whether you have your own cubicle in a shared space, a single office, a storage unit, or even a section of the kitchen, picture how you'll make it your own. What kinds of furnishings and personal productivity tools will you need? Flip through a Staples or Office Depot catalog if you need inspiration and ideas. Personally, I'm pining for a Herman Miller Aeron chair—yes, it's on my board.

Besides furniture and equipment, what color(s) will you paint the walls? Will you put down a rug on the floor, hang artwork on the walls, and hang a bulletin board or whiteboard for notes? How about bookcases, filing cabinets, or other organizing tools? Picture it all, find photos, and plan it out on your vision board. Surround yourself with tools and furnishings that make you happy and, as long as you don't overspend, you'll find you're much more productive.

## Other Rewards

Business owners start their own ventures for myriad reasons. Some want the potential to earn more money. Some know they can do a better job than someone else, such as their current employer, at providing a particular product or service.

Some see a market need and decide to step up and fulfill it. Others desire more schedule flexibility, control, or respect. Do you have reasons beyond money and fame for starting your business? Let's discuss how you can illustrate that on your vision board.

## Control

If having more control—over your life, your day, your workload, or your customers—is one reason you want to own your own company, you're probably in the majority. Most business owners are very clear about how they want their businesses to function.

Some of the ways you can show that on your vision board is to list those areas where you currently don't have control and then find photos, illustrations, and words that show the opposite. Maybe that's a dad arriving home at 5:30 P.M. as promised, or a mom checking her schedule to be sure she can squeeze everything in without being overcommitted. Maybe it's being able to turn down a client or a project. Whatever area you want more control over, you can either find or draw an image of what that looks and feels like.

## Respect

For some business owners, taking control of their own ventures and their own destinies is a way to earn more respect. That respect could be desired from a former boss, a former client, family, or friends. If you're after respect and maybe a little redemption, find photos of the people you want to impress and put them on the board, smiling.

## Summary

- Being clear about the type of company you want to start is helpful in searching for images to reflect your new business. Just knowing you want to be your own boss isn't enough to build a business—you need to know what industry or field you'll work in, too.
- Turn to sources like business magazines, trade journals, industry associations, merchant groups, and competitors for print materials that may have images reflecting the type of business you intend to start.
- Visualizing what you'll do on a daily basis and whom you'll be selling to is another helpful exercise. Picture your customers, products, and services, and the money you'll earn.
- In addition to planning what your business operations will look like, don't overlook your physical workspace. Whether you intend to buy real estate right off the bat to house your new company or, like most entrepreneurs, you're starting out in your garage or basement, devote some space on your board to what your environment will look like.
- Use your vision board to show the type of business you aspire to have, that you fully intend to have. And put aside any negativity or anger that may be fueling your entrepreneurial ambitions.

Want a little help figuring out what to put on your entrepreneurial vision board? Use these questions to zero in on the type of business you'd like to start.

What do you do better than 90 percent of the people you know?

_____

_____

_____

_____

What kinds of activities would you still do even if you weren't paid to do them?

_____

_____

_____

_____

What kind of work experience, including volunteering and part-time jobs, have you had that might be the basis for your own business?

_____

_____

_____

_____

What kind of business would you love to own? Why?

_____

_____

_____

_____

Why haven't you already started it?

_____

_____

_____

_____

What do you need, really, to be able to start your own company?

_____

_____

_____

_____

# CHAPTER 11

# Money, Money, Money

Of all the images people place on their vision boards, money and what can be bought with it have to be the most common. We all want more money, but just wanting money in general isn't enough to cause it to start arriving in your mailbox. You need to get more specific, both about how it's going to come to you and about what you're going to do with it when you have it. In other words, *why* do you want more?

To figure that out, it may be helpful to reflect on your earliest memories of money. What our families teach us about money, good and bad, shapes how we attract and use it later in life. After you understand that, you can design vision boards that counteract some of the money myths you were taught in order to receive all you need.

## What Is Money to You?

Many people develop money associations early that impact how easily they earn and save. For some, money represents a reward for a job well done. For others, it's something they feel entitled to. Sometimes, money can be something that divides a family. There are so many events that become mentally connected with money that it can be difficult to separate the fact from experience—but you need to do just that in order to design a life, and a vision board, that has enough money in it.

### Money Myths

Think about it. Growing up, if you were constantly told that not having enough money was just the way life is, you may have started to believe it and to settle for living with less. If it was suggested that people with money are bad in some way, you might start trying not to hold on to it, for fear that you might be bad.

As you think about some of the things you heard and experienced with respect to money, consider creating illustrations or images that are the exact opposite. So if you were told, "Money doesn't grow on trees," you could draw your own money tree to change your attitude to how easy or difficult it can be to earn more. Maybe you heard, "Money is the root of all evil." If so, you could find images of all the good that money can do to shift your thinking.

Entrepreneurs often hear, "You have to spend money to make money," which is frequently true. However, if you find yourself short of cash too often because it's all been spent, you may want to find images that show a bank account or a wallet full of cash.

## Your Money Challenges

In addition to changing your views about money—how to earn it and hold on to it—you can also use a vision board to overcome how you've treated money. If you've always had a hard time saving money, or if you always seem to hit a plateau in terms of your earnings, your vision board can help you break those limiting scenarios.

Think hard about your relationship with money and what some of your biggest challenges with it are. Then find pictures and statements that reflect your new goals. If saving is difficult for you, think about taking a photo of a savings account balance with several thousand dollars in it. If you've never made more than forty thousand dollars a year, print out a declaration about how much money you will earn this year—an amount that is more than forty thousand dollars.

Sometimes breaking your money patterns has to do with changing your habits. Since most habits take only twenty-one days to change, reminding yourself to do something differently has the power to change your bank account and your lifestyle in only three weeks.

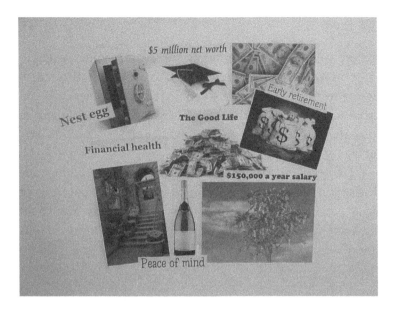

*Put more than photos of cash on your board.*
*Show how those funds will be put to use.*

## Your Annual Income

With never-ending bills arriving on your doorstep each month, it's understandable if your financial focus is on how much money you take home each pay period. Since your paycheck or other monthly income probably has the biggest impact on your buying power and budget, taking aim at increasing its size makes a lot of sense. Similarly, if you're receiving a fixed monthly payment from an outside source, such as a pension distribution, disability payment, or social security check, finding ways to supplement or replace it could be the focus of your money vision board.

## Your Income Goal

Before you can start looking for money or income images to post on your vision board, you need to decide what your goal is. "How much?" and "By when?" are the two questions you need to ask yourself. If your goal is to get a salary increase, you might express your goal in annual terms, such as "a salary of eighty thousand dollars per year."

However, if you're paid on a commission or a sliding-scale basis, you might want to set goals for the next month, or your next review period, whatever length that is. You could set total sales goals in dollars or in number of transactions and then glue them onto your board to remind you daily.

Sonia Miller, author of *The Attraction Distraction: Why the Law of Attraction Isn't Working for You and How to Get Results—Finally!*, uses vision boards on a regular basis and has manifested many things that she posted on her boards, including owning and living on a vineyard, producing award-winning wines, becoming a published writer, acquiring a cottage in the woods to do her work, and, by accident, owning alpacas.

## Your Path to Achievement

Now that you've decided how much money you need to live the life you want, it's time to start pondering how you'll manifest it. Are there activities you've wanted to take up, or get back to, that could generate some extra income? Have you always wanted to run your own business? Do you have a hobby that you could turn into a money-generating sideline?

Asking the universe for a specific amount of money is step one, according to the Law of Attraction, but the clearer you are about where that money might come from, the sooner you'll receive opportunities to earn it. Being proactive shortens the potential window for manifesting your wishes.

## Investing

Another way of approaching the topic of money and how much you have is to set some goals regarding investments. Sure, making more money at a job is always good, but being able to invest and have appreciating assets is even better (of course, the recent recession put quite a damper on much appreciation). Although they don't have to be, investments are generally more long-term oriented—money set aside to grow and be available for the future.

If you're thinking about your future, including your retirement and providing for the next generation, featuring investments on your vision board will get you closer to that goal. And given the ups and downs of the stock market, the more specific you can be about the appreciation you want to see, the better.

### Where to Put Your Money

There are many different types of investment vehicles these days—from traditional interest-bearing checking accounts, certificates of deposit, stocks, and bonds to more sophisticated tools such as real estate investment trusts, stock options, and even peer-to-peer lending. With so many options, it can be hard to decide where to put your money. However, if you have a vision for what kind of portfolio you'd most like to have, or perhaps that your financial adviser has suggested you should aim for, describe that with words and pictures on your vision board.

Will you have a mix of stocks, bonds, and cash, as most conservative investment portfolios do? Or will you invest in riskier tools with a higher payout potential? How do you picture yourself as an investor? That's probably the best question to start with, and then you can begin filling in your portfolio specifics.

### Your Life as an Investor

Your vision board should show what you expect your life will look like with your investments in place. How will it be different with money set aside? Will your lifestyle change? Will your circle of friends shift? Will you do more philanthropic work or volunteer more of your time now that you don't have to work quite as hard? Paint a picture on your board of your life as a well-funded investor.

## Savings

If your more immediate concern is saving for a particular purchase, then your vision board should show all the ways you intend to do that, and the amount you'll amass.

## How Much?

With vision boards, it's important to be specific. Saying you want around 2,500 dollars is too vague. Decide on exactly how much you want and what it's for. If you need 2,498 dollars in order to put a down payment on installing a swimming pool in your backyard this summer, you need to have both the dollar figure and the image of the swimming pool on your board.

Next, as you look at your board, imagine what it will be like to float around in that swimming pool—and how excited and satisfied you'll feel to manifest the 2,498 dollars you need by the first of May.

## *Showing the* How

If you know what you need to do to save, illustrating that on your vision board will reinforce the new kind of saving habit you're trying to develop. If you know going out for lunch every day at work is too costly, show some delicious home-cooked lunches on your board and the amount you can save by packing versus buying. Feel pride every day that you prepare your lunch before work, and imagine all the money going into your bank account. You'll be surprised at how quickly you can bulk up your savings account with help from your vision board.

*An emphasis on foundation building and saving is evident with this vision board.*

## What Are You Worth?

Even if you make a decent income, it's very possible that you're not putting much away for a rainy day. Few of us are, according to the U.S. economists who study savings rates. If you're in this boat, your vision board could be about increasing your net worth, rather than simply boosting your income.

Your net worth is the amount of money you have left over after you subtract what you owe—for things such as a mortgage, a car loan, credit card debt, and any other obligations—from your assets, or what you own. Possible assets include a home, a car, savings accounts, stocks, bonds, or any other things worth a fair amount of money.

## Improving Your Financial Picture

A vision board designed to enhance your financial health through an improved net worth would have images of assets you want to obtain and hold on to. Some of the best investments, historically, have included stocks and bonds, real estate, gold, and similar official financial instruments.

If you have a financial adviser or know one, you might have a conversation about what kinds of financial investments make the most sense for you, depending on your age and financial situation. Then feature those types of investments on your board. For example, the logo of a company whose stock you want to own could work. Or you could include a photo of a handful of certificates of deposit or a deed for a rental property. These are all assets with the potential to appreciate, or increase in value, over time.

## Setting Financial Priorities

Once you have those stocks and bonds or CDs, if you're not clear about holding on to them, your net worth could plunge soon after you obtain them. Unless you want to be right back where you are now in the future, you would be smart to set some new priorities as far as money is concerned.

On your vision board, you might find and feature some statements about saving and amassing wealth—words that inspire you to want to keep attracting more wealth, rather than frittering it away. When your focus is on improving your net worth, your actions should reflect that, such as boosting your income and assets and reducing your expenses and liabilities. The less you owe, the more you're worth. You could include images of paid-off credit-card statements, paid-off student loan statements, or other personal loans that have been taken care of.

> Life coach Hazel Palache has used vision boards regularly for the past six or seven years. On the board she created in January 2008, she added a trip to Europe that she wanted to take, including Rome. She booked a cruise from Rome around Italy, Spain, and France for May 2009. "Having my goals in front of me each day in pictures, as well as written goals, keeps me focused and centered on the bigger picture," she says.

## Your Money Intentions

Sometimes looking at the big picture, your life as a whole, can help you create a vision board that supports your larger life goals. Sure, maybe a few extra dollars each month would make life easier, but what would you really like to accomplish, for yourself and others?

### Maybe It's Not About You

Some of the most successful people in the world recognize that money shouldn't really be a goal, because money is just a tool. It's a resource we need in order to make other things happen.

Although it would be nice to have a big home and a fancy car and be able to take exotic vacations, maybe you also want to make life better for others with the money you aim to attract. What are some of the ways you would use your money to do good deeds? Would you buy a better home for your family in a safer neighborhood? Set up a college fund for your children or grandchildren? Set up a scholarship at your alma mater to help others you don't even know?

How would you like to leave your mark on the world? Would you like to be known for a major environmental improvement project in your area or for running for political office and changing how things are done in your town? Maybe you'd like to start a job-skills program or make it possible for lower-income families to be able to afford their own homes.

What are the things in life that you think shape your ability to be happy and successful, or that will make life better for future generations? When you know what you'd like to do to change the lives of others, you can start looking for images and phrases to put on your board. The name of the nonprofit you plan to start is one idea; the name of the microloan program you're going to initiate for members of your community who want to start their own businesses is another idea. If you can't find an image to represent your large life goals, try to find some words.

Be honest with yourself about your desire for money. If you want to be able to give money away to the less fortunate, make sure it's because you get satisfaction from helping. If you also want to be recognized for it, you'll want to include some images of media coverage or honors to be bestowed on you for your good deeds. Otherwise, you could become *very* frustrated at not receiving the recognition you expected!

## How Life Will Be Different

Another approach to making your dream of helping others come true is to look for images of people who have benefited from your work or of the results of your work. What kinds of pictures would you like to see? Maybe a row of vacant houses cleaned up. If so, take a picture of the houses as they are now and draw over them to show the changes you'll make happen. Maybe your wish is to see your grandchild with a college degree or PhD. Take a picture and add a cap and gown made out of construction paper to represent that achievement.

If larger change is your goal, imagine it and then physically make those changes to a current photo. Use pens, crayons, or colored paper, or overlay other printed photos.

## Summary

- Asking yourself "How much?" and "By when?" is a great starting point for creating a vision board devoted to earning more money.
- Including pictures of financial instruments such as stocks, bonds, CDs, and real estate on your vision board is one way to reinforce the smart money moves you're making.
- Be specific about exactly how much you're trying to set aside and for what purpose. The pur-

pose behind your new savings and investing goals can help reinforce new behavior that hastens the attainment of your goals.

- In addition to thinking about what you and your family need money-wise to lead the life you imagine, think more broadly, too. What philanthropic goals do you have to leave your mark on the world?

Want a little help figuring out what to put on your personal finance vision board? Use these questions to zero in on your financial goals.

What are some of the things you learned about money growing up?

_____

_____

_____

_____

Are there any phrases or money mantras your parents repeated, such as, "Money doesn't grow on trees"?

_____

_____

_____

_____

Were your parents good role models for managing their money?

_____

_____

_____

_____

Did you get the sense that money was difficult to earn or difficult to hold on to? How has that shaped how you handle money?

_____

_____

_____

_____

How much money do you need to earn to have a comfortable lifestyle?

_____

_____

_____

_____

How much money do you need to become financially independent?

_____

_____

_____

_____

# CHAPTER 12

# The Lifestyle You've Only Dreamed Of

Many of us have big dreams—big, expensive dreams. Dreams akin to the lifestyles of the rich and famous, in which by day we lounge poolside at the club, work out with our personal trainers in the afternoon, and spend our evenings at upscale galas and parties, only to come home to well-appointed houses that are perfectly clean. Okay, that's my dream, but you get the idea. A lifestyle vision board shows your life as you would like it to be—the whole picture.

Of course, that vision is different for everyone. Those of us who love our jobs might have a picture to reflect that part of our lives alongside images of things we'd like to improve on—things such as our lawns, our levels of education, and even the labels on our clothing. Those are all elements of our lives that help define our lifestyles.

## Your Dream Home

A common picture that appears on lifestyle vision boards is a home. Whatever your dream is for your future home, that's what you should add to the board. It can be anything from a houseboat to a downtown loft with soaring ceilings, to a lakeside cottage, to a country estate. Where would like to see yourself living?

### Location

If you've always wanted to move west, to Paris, New York City, or a place you fell in love with as a child, now is the time to get specific. You'll have better luck manifesting a condo in Boston's Back Bay, for example, if you post on your board pictures of the area, or even a portion of a map, and the type of property you want to live in. The more specific you can get, the closer your vision will be to becoming a reality.

When your desired location isn't local, scout online for photos or flip through travel guides or vacation planners to pick out some that feel right. However, if you've always loved a house down the street or on the other side of town, it's pretty easy to go take a photo of it to feature on your board. Looking through real estate guides is another great way to find homes that resonate with you.

## More Elbow Room

Maybe a change in location isn't what you're after, but more space is. If that's the case, your vision board should show spacious rooms and homes. Architectural magazines and books can be excellent resources for imagining your next home.

Another approach to featuring a spacious home is to find pictures of rooms that are decorated or arranged as you would like yours to be. Look for pictures that have the type of furniture you want in yours, as well as plenty of space to move around in. Home decorating sites like Houzz and Apartment Therapy and home design magazines can be useful sources for these types of pictures.

Intuitive stylist Emma Lundwall of New York City has used vision boards numerous times, including imagining exactly how she wants her new space to look, "down to the tiniest detail," she says. "I meditate on the vision and make it come alive in my imagination."

She adds, "The key is to be clear, trust, be open to receive the highest good, and let go of attachment to the outcome. I always end by writing, 'This or something better,' as the universe always has much bigger plans for us than we can even imagine."

## Style

Then again, maybe you love your home where it is, but you'd welcome an interior redo. Could you go for a kitchen upgrade or hardwood floors, or a new coat of paint throughout? What's your vision for your home? Find pictures of how you'd like your home to look and feel and post those images on your lifestyle board to begin to make progress toward them.

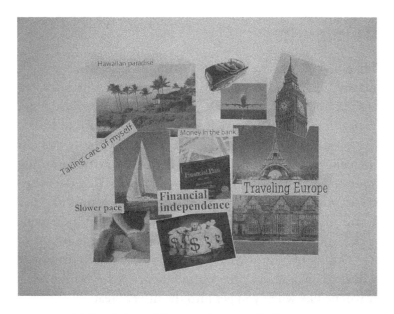

*A lifestyle board features images of what a typical day in your perfect life would look like.*

# Your Transportation

Of course, another big change to your lifestyle could come in the form of a new ride. Since many of us spend so much of our days traveling from one place to another, a new car, truck, or motorcycle would certainly be nice, wouldn't it? Or if jet-setting is more your dream, maybe part ownership in a plush private plane is what you yearn for? What kind of lifestyle are you visualizing?

## Cars, Trucks, and Cycles

Imagine a shiny new sports car sitting in your driveway or a massive pickup truck or SUV in your garage. Whether a car, truck, motorcycle, ATV, RV, or other type of vehicle is on your mind, it's time to give it a place of honor on your board.

In addition to adding a picture of the model you want, in the color you prefer, add pictures of how you envision using your new transportation, too. If you'll be traveling the country in your RV, put some photos of RVs in action on your board. If cruising up the coast on your Harley is more your speed, find some images of that to clarify your intentions.

Adding photos of where and how you'll use your vehicle will also help you imagine yourself there—help you feel what it will be like when you get into the driver's seat.

## Your Own Plane

People who like to travel in style may want to flip through magazines like *Fortune* and *Forbes* in search of photos of private jets that can shuttle them cross-country in pure comfort. Why would you want to deal with the waiting times and security lines of commercial flights if you can fly your own jet?!

Be careful when placing transportation images, such as planes, on your board, or you may suddenly find that you're spending lots of time away from home. The universe may misunderstand your desire for plush accommodations and assume you're looking to fly more. To avoid having a break-neck travel schedule thrust upon you suddenly, you may want to balance that with images of home and family.

## Your Schedule

A big part of envisioning a different lifestyle is picturing how you'll spend your time. Most people would love to do more of some things, perhaps gardening or reading, and less of others, like housecleaning and carpooling. Your vision board is an opportunity to create a different schedule, and lifestyle, for yourself.

### Activities

Before you start brainstorming all the ways you could spend your time, review how you currently spend it. What is your day like? Many people get up, go to work, come back from work, and then maybe work out, clean up, or run errands, followed by dinner, relaxation, and bed, only to go through a similar routine the next day.

If you could remake your day, what would you keep? Would you head to work but for only half a day, followed by volunteering at the library or a local soup kitchen? Or would you ditch work altogether and instead go back to school for an MBA? Maybe school is online, through Duke University's distance-learning program, so you wouldn't even have to leave town.

Picture your perfect day and then translate that into activities you can post on your board.

## Support Staff

Part of the reason many of us are so stressed and our lives are so crammed is that we're doing more than ever before, or trying at least. We have less time to do more work, although the work is just piling up. Heck, it's hard to be us!

Which is why outsourcing some of your obligations is an excellent solution to the overworked state you may currently be in. Why not hand off some of your less pleasant activities to others who would gladly complete them for you?

You've probably heard about major corporations out-sourcing some of their work overseas to people willing to complete it for less. Well, you can do that for other kinds of jobs, too. Outsourcing simply refers to the practice of hand-ing off projects, assignments, or activities to someone else in exchange for pay.

Start by making a list of the to-do items you dread. At home that might include cleaning the house, doing laun-dry, or paying bills, for example. At work, attending meet-ings, running reports, or making presentations may be your dreaded tasks. The key is to find others who are happy to do them for you, starting with finding images of other people doing those activities that you can post on your board.

*Attract others into your life to do what you dislike.*

## Volunteer Work

Many people would love to have the time and money to be able to work less and invest more time in organizations and causes they believe in. They want a lifestyle that permits them to spend less time earning a paycheck and more time pitching in at an important event or rally.

### Your Participation

Wanting to commit more time to volunteering is a great goal, but until you can get more specific about what that looks like, it will be difficult to add that physical image to your vision board.

By "be more involved," do you mean that you'll donate more money each year to support a particular cause? Or do you mean you'll be present at more board or committee meetings, or be more hands-on in terms of fundraisers and special events?

What does that involvement look like to you, and to others? Picture it and then find images, maybe from past events, and put yourself in the thick of things on your board.

## Where You'll Pitch in

Although most people give of themselves in their local communities, other people—maybe you—look for ways to contribute in communities that are even needier than their own. These efforts to help out might follow a national disaster, such as Hurricane Maria in Puerto Rico, or even an international crisis, such as after the tsunami in Indonesia.

If you've always wanted to build a Habitat for Humanity house, for example, put that on your vision board. But think, too, about where you most want to build it. Do you want to pitch in downtown or in another part of the state or country? Are you drawn to any particular area or country? Make sure your vision reflects where you expect to be doing good work.

## What You Aspire to Do

Some people picture themselves helping others with particular types of tasks, such as learning to speak English or learning to read. Others are more interested in tackling infrastructure-type projects, like clearing brush or planting a community garden.

What types of charitable work are you most in tune with? That's really the question you need to ask yourself before you start planting seeds of opportunity with your vision board.

## Education

Although a college degree is now considered the standard for getting a job, many Americans have only a high school diploma or have only completed some high school coursework. Completing high school or earning a college degree or an advanced degree is a popular goal that a vision board can help support. Start by deciding what your ultimate goal is and then put it on your board.

### College Degree

For many people who had to get off the college track due to family or work obligations, it's tough to get back on. But if earning a college degree has been on your life's to-do list for a while, add it to your vision board.

Is there a particular college or university you aspire to study at? Is there a professor you're dying to study with, or a particular major you're committed to? Put on your board images of college life, words describing the types of courses you'll take, the grades you'll get, and what you'll end up with when you're done.

### Vocational Training

If you've been contemplating a job change for a while, or even for a few months, some vocational, or skills, training may be just what you need. Gaining new skills and earning a certificate can be the start of a whole new line of work for you.

One place to check is the association for the industry you want to enter, which you can find in the massive *Encyclopedia of Associations*. You can find it at most major libraries. Many associations can suggest training programs or starting points for entry into that field.

## Study for Pleasure

Earning a college degree isn't the only reason to go back to school, however. A love of learning, or an interest in a particular subject area, is a potent draw back to the classroom. For example, you may want to learn all there is to know about ancient Greece, without having to use it as part of a job.

If you're attracted to the studious atmosphere of a college or university campus but feel no need to get on a degree track, consider adding to your board the names of courses that appeal to you. Or show pictures of a more leisurely pace on a college campus to reflect your different outlook on studying.

# Work

We probably spend more time at work, on the job, than on any other outside activity. It's an important part of our lives and, in many cases, it defines our identities for many years.

That doesn't mean it always has to be that way, however. If you're ready for a change and picture a lifestyle with a different employer, different role, or different schedule, it's time to put that on your vision board.

## How Invested Are You?

One big lifestyle shift can occur when you scale back your time spent at work. Deciding that your personal and career balance is out of whack can result in big changes, but first you need to decide how big a role you want your job to play in your life.

Some individuals love their jobs and see no problem working far more than forty or fifty hours a week—they love it! And that's fine. I probably wouldn't recommend putting images on your vision board that would push you to work upward of fifty hours a week, but to each his own. On the other hand, many employees report being willing to give up part of their paycheck in order to take more time to themselves. If that's where you are, it's time to put more emphasis on what you'll do outside of work when you have all this free time, because your vision board is going to help you figure out what really lights you up.

## What Will You Do?

If you would prefer to work fewer hours per week, find images that reflect a more leisurely pace. If what you really want is more weeks of vacation, consider posting a mini calendar with several weeks blocked off when you'll be out of the office on vacation. Be sure to show how you'll fill all that vacation time, whether you spend more time on hobbies, with friends and family, or traveling the world.

Television producer Nicole Dunn uses vision boards to manifest her life goals. In 2008, she earned a nomination for a daytime Emmy but says, "I wasn't specific enough [she wanted a win!]; this year I will be." She has also manifested her dream boyfriend, now soon-to-be husband, and a spot on the cover of *Kiplinger's Personal Finance*. "I talk a lot about the boards, my vision, and the projects to get my momentum going to the universe," she explains. And it works.

# First Steps

Posting pictures and phrases on your board to get external energy moving in your direction is what vision boards are designed to do, but to jump-start some lifestyle shifts, you might spend a little time thinking about what you can do to encourage those shifts. The more proactive you are, the more quickly opportunities may come your way.

## Resources to Get Started

What is it you need or you can do right now to set some changes in motion? Do you need friends to bolster your confidence to ask for an assistant at work to reduce your workload? Do you need more money in order to be able to scale back the number of jobs you're currently holding? Do you need more childcare help so you can go back to school? What is it that will make the biggest lifestyle change possible?

## Timetable and Milestones

Figuring out how to initiate change is huge, but attaching deadlines and targets is even more energizing, because then you'll have a specific date or timeline within your goal must be met. You can't just work on change indefinitely; you need to make certain things happen by such-and-such a date. There's nothing better than a little accountability, even on vision boards.

# Summary

- To change your lifestyle, start by imagining your perfect day, and then take steps to get rid of activities you don't like, while adding those you do.
- Where you live plays a big role in your lifestyle and how you feel about yourself and your life. If you picture yourself in a different location, a different type of home, or a different-size home, make sure you have images that reflect those changes posted on your vision board.
- Think about how you'd prefer to spend your time if money were no object, and then post or draw images on your vision board showing your desired lifestyle.
- Perhaps there are some chores you would love to hand off to someone else. Find images of people doing what you dislike, whether it's cleaning, gardening, driving, bill paying, or grocery shopping, and post them on your board.

Want a little help figuring out what to put on your lifestyle vision board? Use these questions to zero in on what makes sense for you and the life you want to live.

You've just won ten million dollars in the lottery. Describe your new lifestyle.

_____

_____

_____

_____

What are the first three things you would buy?

_____

_____

_____

_____

If you had all the money you ever needed, how would your life be different?

_____

_____

_____

_____

How would it be the same?

_____

_____

_____

_____

Who would you share your wealth with?

_____

_____

_____

_____

# CHAPTER 13

# Family and Friends

People enter our lives on a daily basis, often for only a passing moment, and we move on. But people with whom we have a biological or an emotional attachment stay with us longer. Some we have an ongoing, healthy relationship with, others perhaps only an occasional interaction, and a few we rarely see. Frequency of communication doesn't always reflect the depth or impact of that relationship, however.

Healthy, happy, and supportive relationships can transform our lives and our potential for the future, while negative entanglements can interfere with our success and even set us back on the road to our goals.

Fortunately, you can use a vision board to help you define the type of relationships you want to have with the important people in your life.

## The Relationship You Wish You Had

No matter how much we love our family members and our friends, rarely are those relationships without challenges or misunderstandings. Sometimes, those misunderstandings can taint the potentially wonderful connections that make our lives that much fuller and more satisfying.

With focus and reflection, you can begin to see patterns in how you interact that can help you improve your relationships. Your vision board can help.

### In a Perfect World...

...everyone would get along and there would be peace and love among all those who are close to you. Unfortunately, rarely is this possible. That doesn't mean that you have to throw up your hands and give in to the dissension. No, you don't have to participate in the drama at all, but then you'd be cutting yourself off from those you love. So what are your options?

First, describe how you'd like your friends and family to behave around you. How is that different from how they behave now? What are the words that describe your interactions with them—in your dreams, that is? For example, are they supportive, encouraging, and complimentary? Or maybe interested, warm, and generous?

With those words in mind, search for images you can place on your vision board. You might find photos of friends having fun or photos that suggest the sense of camaraderie and joy that you may want your family to share. Or if you have photos of your family and friends behaving the way you'd like them to, use those instead.

Vision board photos don't have to be literal. That is, the images you select and place on the board don't have to exactly mirror images of people and situations in your life that you'd like to change. You can also use images that suggest feelings to you, such as calm or excitement. It doesn't matter what physical things are shown as long as you react to the image and feel the desired sensation. For example, a setting sun over a lake might be relaxing, and a photo of a crowd dancing at a nightclub might make you feel excited and happy.

## How Will You Change the Dynamic?

Now that you're clear about how you want things to change with your loved ones, what can and will you do about it?

The first question to ask yourself is whether there is anything you can do. It's possible there isn't. Sometimes long-held beliefs and feelings simply can't be changed, by anyone. But maybe your situation can be reversed or improved. Think about that.

Then recall situations that have occurred in the past in which you believe a different outcome could have been obtained. What would have needed to happen? For example, when your cousin started drinking at lunchtime, could someone have cut him off to avoid the subsequent altercation that always comes at family gatherings? Those types of shifts and changes are what you need to place on your board to help remind you of different approaches you can take to achieve new responses and reactions from those around you.

## How Will You Feel?

You should also include images that indicate how you will feel when your friends and family are behaving the way you would like. Are you less stressed? Less worried? Less angry? Happier? Relieved? Loved? Appreciated? How would you describe how you would feel if everyone were only loving and supportive, rather than how they are now? Capture that in word and image, and place them on your board to push the process along.

Keep in mind that you are the only person you can truly control. You can control how you think and behave, and how you react to others. So some of the images on your vision board could reflect new behavior that you're committed to adopting to facilitate changes in others.

*You can't force others to change, but you can change and therefore cause a shift in how others react.*

# Communication

Sometimes, the frustrations or disappointments that arise in relationships are the result of a lack of communication or miscommunication. How, when, and why we take time to communicate with one another affect the quality of our interactions and our responses. For example, if you hear from a friend only when she needs money or from your brother only when he needs to vent about a situation in which he's involved, you'll begin to wish you hadn't picked up the phone. You associate the person with the negative news that inevitably follows.

Now is your chance to turn those conversations and phone calls around and make them enjoyable for everyone. It all starts with your intention and your vision of the exchange.

## "You Never Call"

Relationships develop and change over time. The more interactions you share, the more connected—or disconnected—you can become, based on the quality and content of those interactions. But frequency also plays a role here, because you can have a close relationship with someone, yet feel slighted because he or she is never the one to suggest you go grab a drink or pick up the phone.

Because most relationships consist of a give-and-take, or a back-and-forth, exchange, it gets tough to maintain a relationship if one of you fails to communicate (maybe you've heard this during a plea from your mom to check in more often).

If you'd like to improve your own communication frequency, or that of those around you, use your vision board to indicate how often you'd like to hear from or get together with those you are close to. Would you like to talk with your best friend daily? Would you like your family to come to your house for Thanksgiving every other year? How often do you want to hear from your family and friends? Decide what you'd like to aim for initially and place that target on your vision board, either as an image or a written goal.

## Phone, Text, Email, Gorillagram?

How and where your communication with family and friends occurs are also important to examine. Would you like to hear more from friends by phone and receive less email from family members, who have placed you on their email distribution lists and send you lame joke after lame joke? Would you like to dial back the family get-togethers to make time to hang out with your girlfriends every once in a while?

There is no right or wrong approach here, but you need to decide your preferred mode of communication and then put that on your vision board so you can encourage more of that kind of communicating and less of what you're getting now. If you want more phone calls, find pictures of telephones. If you want more emails or instant messages, find or take pictures of those kinds of communiqués. If you want more interaction on social media, include some logos of Snapchat or Instagram. And if you want more face-to-face time, see if you can dig up photos of you and your friends or family together and place those on your board. Imagine the best scenario and then find images that show that.

Kristina Kolerich grew up on the South Side of Chicago in a wonderful Italian neighborhood steeped in tradition. It was expected that she would grow up, marry someone from the neighborhood, and live with her children only a few blocks from her parents. Yet she knew this was not her destiny, and from a young age created what she called motivation boards to show her a different path. Her dream was to become a broadcast journalist, and despite her parents' telling her repeatedly it was okay to give up and become a secretary, Kristina stayed focused on her dreams. She did achieve a career in broadcast journalism and reached the network level in her hometown. Today she has her own company, an oceanfront home, and a nice car, and is financially secure. "I visualized my life and made it come true," she says.

# Time Spent Together

At various points in our lives, it's tough to find time for everyone we love. Somehow we do, though, because they're important to us. If folks you care about just haven't managed to find the time to see you in a long time, use your vision board to bring them back around.

## Making Get-Togethers a Regular Occurrence

You know that your friends and family love you, but if you'd like to see them more often than you do now, it's time to find images that will bring them back into your life on a regular basis. Look for photos of you and them together in various places and situations and add them to your vision board. The

CREATE YOUR VISION BOARD

more frequent those photos appear, the more energy you'll be investing in attracting those near and dear to you.

If time is also a factor—you'd like those activities to be more than a five-minute chat—you'll want to look for images that show you and the person or people together for a whole evening or a whole day. Maybe you'll have a series of pictures of large families gathered around the dinner table, helping clean up in the kitchen, enjoying dessert on the front porch, and hanging out watching TV in the living room. Or you could aim for a family picnic in the park, with photos of kids playing football, the men stereotypically gathered around the barbecue grill, women chatting or playing volleyball, or of other group activities you'd enjoy.

## Where Will You Meet?

Sometimes it's not the frequency or length of visits that can be a source of contention, but *where* you get together. Do you always go to your friend's house to watch the game, or does your friend always come to your house for drinks? If you're in a rut that you'd like to get out of, you need images of your friends or family in other locations on your vision board, preferably with you in the picture, too.

So, if you want your family to come to your home on Christmas Eve, find or draw pictures of your home on Christmas Eve and put photos of your family there, having fun. Or if you want your girlfriends to get babysitters and come out with you to an adults-only dinner, create a collage that shows that experience.

## "What Will We Do?"

Speaking of experiences, wouldn't it be great if you could do something different with your gang? Maybe take a trip together or plan a road trip to a friend's house several hours away? Maybe you'd like to go to a concert or go skiing? Think of your ideal activity and use your vision board to make it a reality.

## Planning Fun Activities

Doing something new and different doesn't have to involve a long and expensive trip. Plan a block or neighborhood party or schedule a night of bowling for you and your friends to get everyone out of the house and doing something a little out-of-the-ordinary. Maybe you'd like to take a nice boat ride on a local river or hike a nearby bluff.

Whatever the activity you'd like to engage in, decide on it, picture it, and then look for images that relate to it to use on your vision board.

Make sure you are specific when placing images on your board, or you may attract an opportunity that isn't quite what you expected. For example, if you want all your friends to join you for a Friday-night barbecue at your house, make sure you feature photos of those friends, your home, and your grill filled with steaks. Because if you don't include all your friends, or you don't show your house or an evening barbecue, you may get a night of drinking with only a few of your buddies. Be careful what you wish for.

## Planning a Trip

While get-togethers close to home are easier to make happen, maybe what you'd like is a fun weekend of snow tubing, going to a spa, or floating down the Brandywine River outside Philadelphia. As you start putting together the details and throwing the idea out to your friends or family, create a vision board that shows all the pieces that are important to you—the friends you want to come along, a group doing what you want to do, lots of laughter, and anything else you think is important to the trip.

# What You Are Willing to Do

Improving and shaping your relationships with people who are important to you take effort—on your part and theirs. Whether it's a matter of making time, being less critical of others, participating more in the conversation, or being willing to do what others have planned, you may have to change your thoughts and behavior in order to strengthen those bonds.

## A New You

No, you don't have to become a new person in order to get along with your friends and family. If you do, your friends aren't really your friends (your family, that's another story—you're stuck with them). But given the kinds of changes you'd like to see in how, when, and where you and your buddies communicate and congregate, what are you willing to do to make those get-togethers occur? What are you willing to do to make them more enjoyable? Or what are you willing to do to make them happen?

Think about the lengths to which you are willing to go to get your gang together and have fun. How about if you volunteered to organize and host a weekly poker game or book club, shouldering the responsibility for inviting everyone and having them over? Or maybe you could invite a group to become part of a supper club that rotates among three or four homes each month for dinner. If you're willing to step up and make some social gatherings happen, find images that show that kind of effort and place them on your board, along with images of successful gatherings.

Megan Riley's family used vision boards as family projects when she was growing up. They would talk about a family vacation they wanted to take and then begin a board to capture where they wanted to go and what they wanted to do. Over dinners they would refine their desired vacation and then manifest the money, airplane tickets, and hotels "seemingly out of thin air," she says. The most profound trip happened when Megan was twelve, when the family traveled to the Cayman Islands to snorkel, go treasure hunting in sunken ships, play on the beach, and order lots of room service. When they got home and looked at the vision board again, they realized they had done everything on it.

## What Are Your Limits?

Of course, few of us are willing to do absolutely anything to achieve peace in our families or among our friends. We all have our limits. What are yours?

It's important to know what you are not willing to do so that you don't end up feeling taken advantage of. Your goal is to create harmony and increase the amount of time you spend together, but where do you draw the line?

Now, do not start finding pictures of those limits to place on your board—what you'll end up doing is attracting those opportunities. Instead, find pictures of what you are willing to do. For example, maybe you are willing to travel to a reunion in Texas but not in Florida. So find a Texas bumper sticker and put that on your board. Or maybe you'd share a room at Disney World with three friends but not five. So find a picture of four friends at Disney World.

Creating more harmonious, enjoyable relationships with family and friends can have lasting benefits that impact other aspects of your life, too. You may be surprised at how a more fulfilling social life brings new potential romantic partners into your circle of friends or creates networking opportunities that lead to a new job or business. Or how patching things up with a sibling or an in-law can reduce your stress level and help repair relationships with other family members. Improved relationships tend to have a domino effect on several aspects of our lives. Most of all, being happier and less stressed about the people closest to you will help you recognize all the good you already have in your life.

## Summary

- If you can pinpoint specific things you would change about your friends and family to make your relationships with them stronger, you can use a vision board to make those changes a reality.
- Sometimes, communication—either too much or too little—is at the source of disharmony. Picture the frequency you'd like and then look for

images to apply to your vision board that reflect those changes.

- If the frequency and tone of communication are great but you feel like you never get to see those close to you, consider adding pictures of activities you'd like to enjoy with your gang—maybe a night out on the town or a family reunion out of town.
- In some cases, change needs to happen for everyone to get along and have a good time. What are you unwilling to do? Set your limits so you avoid frustrating yourself and others.

Want a little help figuring out what to put on your family and friends vision board? Use these questions to zero in on what makes sense for you and the relationships you'd like to have with those important to you.

How would you describe your relationship with your parents?

_____

_____

_____

_____

How would you like it to be different?

_____

_____

_____

_____

What are your favorite family memories?

_____

_____

_____

_____

How have your relationships with family members changed through the years?

_____

_____

_____

_____

What can you do, if anything, to improve them?

_____

_____

_____

_____

What would your family members need to do to improve them?

_____

_____

_____

_____

# CHAPTER 14

# Romantic Relationship

Although most of us focus a lot of time and attention on money and material things that make life more comfortable, the truth is that personal relationships—especially romantic connections—are far more important to and powerful for many people. When you have someone special to share experiences, travel, and conversation with, life gets a whole lot more satisfying.

Of course, you probably already know this, but if you haven't yet found your soul mate, you may want to create a vision board to attract him or her into your life.

## When You're Together

Logically, you might assume you should start your search for a mate by describing the type of person you're seeking. Not here. You'll do that in a minute, but for a vision board to attract the person who will put the biggest smile on your face and make you feel truly cherished and optimistic about the future, you need to start with how you will feel when you're around your future romantic partner.

### How You Spend Your Time Together

It may be tough to imagine what love will feel like with someone, so start by picturing what you'll do when you're together. What kinds of activities are your favorites? Will you head to the theater for evenings of culture, or are bars more to your liking? Maybe you're an outdoors lover, and hikes in the woods or trail rides on horseback are more your idea of romance.

When you have an idea of what you'd most like to be doing with your partner, look for images that show those types of activities, such as snowmobiling, waterskiing, traveling, or watching movies by the fireside.

After being single for many years and doing plenty of dating, Reverend Jeri Murphy had a clear idea of what she did and did not want in a relationship. So in the spring of 2001 she created a vision board for her ideal partner. Her central affirmation was, "I am thriving in my passionate, loving relationship," and on the board she posted pictures of couples doing many of her favorite things together. She then hung it in her bathroom vanity area, where she would be sure to see it daily. She met her sweetheart, Richard, in 2004, and realized a few months later that he personified every phrase and picture she had placed on her board. They'll soon celebrate five happy years together.

## That Lovin' Feeling

Most important of all, however, is the feeling in your heart when you're together. Can you describe it? Are you excited? Energized? Optimistic? Do you feel more attractive? Sexy? Confident? Calm? And how do you behave around others? Are you kinder? More considerate?

It's often said that we behave differently when we're in love. If you believe that could be true for you, picture what that change looks like. Do you smile more? Are you more sociable or maybe more concerned about your appearance? Now find images that match that and place them on your board to attract those feelings.

## Defining Your Ideal Mate

Now that you have the feeling down pat, let's get more specific about what you're looking for. What kind of person do you want in your life as a significant other? The more specific you can be, the better your odds of attracting that exact kind of person.

## Appearance

Although most of us will say that appearance is not as important as personality or behavior, what people look like on the outside is what we naturally react to first. Although we may be willing to overlook certain features once we get to know the person better, it's always nice when you can find someone who is immediately attractive to you both on the inside and out.

*When your focus is on attracting a romantic partner, your board should include pictures of your ideal mate.*

So, what are some physical features you find attractive? Make a list, if you can, thinking about any or all of these characteristics:

- Hair—color, length, style
- Face—beard, mustache, clean-shaven, skin tone
- Eyes—color, glasses
- Body—petite, muscular, fit, curvaceous
- Height—tall, same height, shorter
- Other—clean hands and nails, style of dress

When you have a mental picture of your ideal mate, you'll have an easier time finding pictures of similar body types and facial features to paste to your board.

Victoria Loveland-Coen created a vision board more than 16 years ago and included on it a picture of a beautiful wedding ring. It had a unique marquise-shaped diamond in the center with diamond baguettes on the side that flared out like a bow. At the time, she was dating someone but they weren't serious. But when they did decide to marry, she received a ring with the very marquise-shaped diamond she had placed on her vision board. She still has the ring and the husband.

## Personality

With the mental picture of your future partner in your head, what does he or she act like? What are some words you would use to describe your mate? Here are some examples:

- Friendly
- Shy
- Confident
- Genuine
- Sincere
- Warm
- Outgoing
- Charismatic
- Bubbly
- Aloof
- Intelligent
- Funny
- Serious
- Caring

Maybe there are other words to describe how he or she relates to others. Write or type them and put them on your board.

Since the words you're using relate to someone you're searching for, consider putting them in quotes, since you're using them to describe someone else, not you. Pretend that you're telling the universe what you want.

## Temperament

Along the same lines as personality is temperament, or how people react when they are emotional. It's part emotion, part temper, really.

Are you looking for someone who can be passionate about his or her convictions and opinions, who can get swept up into fighting for what he or she strongly believes? Perhaps someone who fights hard for something wanted (meaning verbally, not physically)? Or are you after someone who is more subdued—maybe someone who remains calm no matter what is happening around him or her?

## Goals

As you search for someone special, right now you probably will be more concerned with getting along on a daily basis than with future goals. Yet before you get too involved, it would be smart to double-check that your life goals are in sync, which means you'd be wise to put your life goals on your vision board, too. Goals might include:

- Marriage
- Children
- Travel
- Retirement
- Buying a home
- Finishing a degree

What are some other goals you've set for yourself? State what they are upfront so that you and anyone important in your life can support your efforts.

## Priorities

Sometimes our life goals reflect our priorities, and sometimes they don't. For example, a goal may be to retire early, if you can, but a bigger priority may be having children. To make sure you and your mate are in sync, you may want to talk about which goals are essential and which are lower down the list.

You can communicate those priorities by including them on your vision board, perhaps in a larger size than less important goals, like joining a local country club.

*By making sure that images of your most important goals are larger, they will naturally catch your attention more often—you'll focus on them more strongly.*

## Lifestyle

Another consideration as you're keeping watch for your sweetie is the lifestyle you'd like to have together. If you're a city gal and he's a diehard country lover, you may have a little trouble finding middle ground. Better to know that upfront.

So, think about your preferred lifestyle. Does it include…

- Loft living downtown?
- A bungalow in the burbs?
- A country homestead?
- An RV in which you travel the country?
- Traveling between seasonal homes?
- Living abroad?
- Joining a commune?

Of course, there are other options, too, but these should get you started in thinking about where you'd most like to live.

If your dream is to be in another city with your partner, it's very possible your future love is already there. Rather than continuing to look in your current location in the hopes of convincing that someone special to move, why not move yourself and start looking there? Start that process by adding a picture of your desired home to your vision board to draw you there.

## Your Future Together

Once you find your romantic equal, what kind of future are you envisioning for the two of you? Are you looking for someone to date and have fun with, or are you searching for someone to settle down with? The future you desire and describe on your vision board will shape the type of person drawn into your life.

## Live Together or Get Married?

If you're not ready to think about marriage yet but you'd like to have someone in your life in a significant way, your goal may be to find someone to live with. You might show this on your vision board by featuring pictures of loving couples together at home, minus the wedding ring.

On the other hand, if it is your goal to be married, make sure you communicate that on your vision board. You don't just want a partner; you want a spouse.

Images you could use that make that clear include a wedding ring or set of rings, a wedding gown, a bride and groom, and a picture of a church or beautiful location.

In addition to applying wedding-related photos, feel free to use actual products, like invitations, pieces of a veil, and faux flowers. The more realistic your vision board components, the easier it will be for your brain to see the event occurring.

## Do You Want Children?

Depending on your stage in life, children may be too far in the future to contemplate, or you may be beyond that stage of life, perhaps looking forward to grandchildren. Or maybe you simply don't have any interest in being a parent. However you are feeling about children is perfectly fine—no pressure.

But if this is a subject on which you have definite preferences, you'll want to be clear on those upfront so that you attract a romantic partner who is of like mind.

If you have no interest in giving birth to or adopting children, make sure they don't appear on your vision board. If they do, your brain may interpret the image to mean you want children of your own, and it will devote energy to attracting them for you.

## Your Search Begins

In addition to putting images of your desired partner on your vision board, it's always a good idea to take action, too. The more energy you devote to your goals—mental, physical, and emotional—the more quickly you will achieve them.

Since you've described your future partner in fairly detailed fashion already, consider where you'll look to meet him or her. Your vision board will help bring you in close proximity to him or her, but by stepping out into new territory, you may hasten your introduction.

So where is your love likely to be found? Consider your description of him or her, including his or her likes and dislikes, hobbies, interests, and lifestyle. Then spend a little time in those places to see whom you run across.

If you're looking for someone who enjoys certain pastimes, how about starting your hunt based on those? Or if he or she runs in certain circles—whether that includes charity balls or motorcycle rallies—consider how you can join in or watch from the sidelines.

Your vision board is your guide and your reflection of what you're working toward, but a little effort on your part to be in the right place at the right time can only help.

## Summary

- Having a clear idea of what your future mate looks like can help you sort through the many romantic candidates out there.
- Think about—maybe even make a list of—what your love looks like, acts like, and enjoys doing.
- Looking ahead to your future together, be sure your goals and priorities, such as marriage and a family, match up with any potential partners'.
- While your vision board will help you identify potential partners, the more you can do to help your vision of a romantic partner appear, the more quickly he or she will appear.

Want a little help figuring out what to put on your romance vision board? Use these questions to zero in on what you want in a soul mate.

Describe your soul mate: what he or she looks like, acts like, enjoys, and so on.

_____

_____

_____

_____

What physical features are you most attracted to?

_____

_____

_____

_____

What are big turn-offs for you?

_____

_____

_____

_____

What kinds of activities and interests do you have that you'd like to share with a romantic partner?

_____

_____

_____

_____

Are there activities you're not currently involved in that you'd like to participate in with someone else?

_____

_____

_____

_____

Describe a typical day spent with your partner. What do you do with and say to each other?

_____

_____

_____

_____

# CHAPTER 15

# A Healthier Lifestyle

One of the biggest ways to improve your life is to improve your health, which starts with changing how you take care of yourself. Whether you want to slim down, bulk up, improve your eating habits, or quit smoking, a vision board can help remind you of the healthier habits you're in the process of adopting. In the short term, a vision board can get you past that nicotine craving or the temptation of the chocolate cake offered for dessert, and in the long term, a vision board can transform your life as well as extend it.

As with any desired change, creating a vision board that represents your future health is a smart first step. And if you're not sure about the healthy changes you need to make, start by asking your doctor. He or she can guide you and indicate what types of physical activity and diet alterations are healthy and which are dangerous. Whatever you do, don't put your symptoms or health concerns on your vision board—you'll only fixate on them and make them worse.

## Losing Weight

Whether you've always had a bit of extra cushioning or carrying some extra weight is a relatively new state for you, a vision board can help you slim down.

The first step is deciding exactly how much you want to lose. The goal of "losing weight" isn't specific enough to yield any results, but stating that you'll lose fifteen pounds or reach a weight of 180 pounds will get you somewhere. You should also find photos of people who are near your ideal weight to place on your board.

Sometimes seeing beautiful, trim people on your vision board isn't enough to spark a change in you, because you don't yet believe that *you* can be that weight. If this is the case for you, glue a photo of your head on someone else's body so you can start to envision yourself at that weight.

### Eating Right

Everyone knows that to lose weight, you need to cut your caloric intake by eating less or eat the same and get more physical activity. However, sometimes it's not simply about eating smaller quantities—it's also about eating different foods. If you love fatty foods like fried chicken, hamburgers, cake, and ice cream, replacing them with fruits, vegetables, and lower-fat fare will have almost immediate results.

On your vision board, you may want to remind yourself of your new healthy eating habits by applying pictures of healthier foods. Seeing all those beautiful photos of delicious apples, broccoli, and raspberries will help you stay focused on the healthful foods that will get you to your goal.

*Images of healthy foods can keep you from*
*straying to unhealthy options.*

## Exercising

The other component of a healthy lifestyle is exercise. Some people have physical-labor jobs that give them a built-in workout. However, most people today work indoors, rarely lifting more than a few pieces of paper. If that describes you,

you probably already know the importance of adding some cardiovascular activity to your day.

Before jumping into a massive exercise program that may be hard to stick with, consider the types of physical activities you enjoy. Here are some ideas to get you started:

- Walking
- Swimming
- Aerobic exercise
- Running
- Lifting weights
- Skiing
- Kickboxing
- Playing on a team
- Practicing yoga
- Taking a Pilates class
- Using kettlebells

Pick a few of the types of activities you like, commit to participating in them regularly, and then put photos of them on your vision board. Be specific about what you'll do and when, too, such as running one mile a day, five days a week, or exercising for at least forty-five minutes three times a week. Seeing someone running a marathon, participating in a triathlon, or doing yoga will remind you of what you should be doing to get into shape. But start with small changes, both so you don't injure yourself and so you don't lose momentum by trying to do too much too fast. You can use your vision board to introduce new changes to your healthier lifestyle and to note improvements along the way.

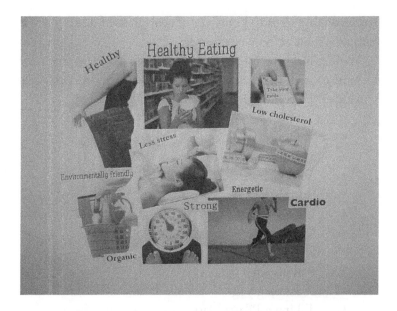

*Whether your goal is more energy, a slimmer fig-
ure, or disease prevention, a vision board can
remind you how to live a healthier lifestyle.*

## Seeing Results

Unfortunately, it does take some time—generally about four
weeks—before you start seeing big results from your healthy
living. When you do start seeing results, consider adding
updated photos of yourself to your board to inspire you.
Including a "before" picture along with "after" pictures as
you become fitter can be inspirational.

In addition to pictures of yourself on your vision board,
add words and numbers that reflect quantitative goals you've
set for yourself. You might put the time you want to beat
in your next running race, the weight you want to be in six

months, or that inspirational quote your coach keeps throwing out when you want to quit. Sometimes numbers and words are just as powerful as visual images.

## Overcoming Disease

Sometimes it takes the diagnosis of a disease or serious health problem to wake us up and push us to make significant changes to our lifestyles. If that's where you are, your vision board can help you make those changes and see the future, healthier you.

### What You Can Do

Ask your doctor what you can do on a daily basis, no matter how small, to improve your condition. Whether you've been diagnosed with Type 2 diabetes or high cholesterol, or you're battling breast cancer, you can use a vision board to initiate healthy changes in your lifestyle. Start by determining what you need to change. Should you reduce the stress in your life? Should you stop eating sugar? Should you make sure you take your medication on time? Get to bed before 10:00 P.M.? Stay away from negative people? Eat more raw produce? Take more walks?

Whatever your health condition, your doctor will surely have recommendations for what you can do to improve your health. If you have diabetes, for example, monitoring your glucose level regularly is one important step that you could show on your vision board, as well as eating healthy foods and getting exercise. Or if you're recovering from surgery, you could look for images of people participating in recommended activities or doing doctor-sanctioned exercises, such as swimming, if that is the case with you.

Find out what you need to do, find images of people doing those things, and post them on your board. Seeing them regularly on your board will help to make them part of your daily life and routine, which will make the changes easier to adjust to.

## Focus on the Positive

Fighting a disease or chronic condition can be scary, and if you let it, it can sap your energy and steal all your attention. To avoid focusing so much on yourself and your ills, use a vision board to remind yourself of the progress you're making and where you're headed. Look to the future if the present isn't so enjoyable and use your vision board to remind you of what you hold dear and why you're working to get better.

Donna Hartley used her vision board not to manifest a new car or house but to have a successful open-heart surgery to replace her aortic valve. Donna and her daughter Mariah created a board and put on it the words "Perfect Health. Perfect Surgery. Perfect Recovery." Donna looked at it every morning and night. The surgery was a great success, and Donna's only regret was forgetting to put on her board that the surgery would be pain-free. Now on her vision boards she makes sure to cover all her bases, with very clear words and pictures.

# Quitting Smoking

If you smoke, one of the best things you can do for your body, your life, and those around you is to quit. You probably already knew that, but nicotine is a drug. It's tough to give up tobacco products, but if you've decided this is what you want to do, a vision board can help keep them at bay.

## Getting Past the Urge to Smoke

For most smokers, it can be hard to imagine not having cigarettes or cigars to turn to. They become part of your life, almost like a friend. But the truth is that they are shortening your life and the lives of those around you.

To help you stay away from tobacco products, remind yourself of what you're missing when you smoke. Do you have trouble walking any distance, or running? Are you not allowed to have your nieces and nephews in your home because you smoke? Put images of the people you love on your vision board, as well as the things you'd like to do but have trouble with as a smoker.

## Getting Help

Giving up smoking is a big step, and few people can make it alone—vision board or not. If you know people or organizations that can help you, put them on your vision board. And if there are people who believe you have the strength to quit—who need you to quit, such as your children or grandchildren—be sure to put them on your vision board, too, since you'll have many more years to spend with them if you can become a nonsmoker.

## Getting Pregnant

Our bodies don't always perform the way we expect or want them to, including when couples are trying to get pregnant. While we can't control conception, both men and women can do some things to help their bodies get ready for the woman to become pregnant.

Jeanna Gabellini has had the same vision board up for about six years. On it she has included several pictures of an amazing pregnancy in which she looks "hot." As a result, "I had the *best* nine months," says Jeanna. She stayed active thanks to yoga, which she took up because of the pictures on her vision board.

Your gynecologist is certainly the best source of advice regarding things you can do to increase your odds of becoming pregnant, but some healthy steps you can take to improve your overall health include:

- Quitting smoking
- Changing your diet
- Cutting back on alcohol
- Reducing your stress level
- Gaining a little weight if you are underweight

In addition to adding photos of pregnant women to your vision board, be sure to show images of babies, since having a baby is your ultimate objective.

**Men can also make changes to improve their fertility, such as:**

- Quitting smoking
- Changing your diet
- Cutting back on alcohol
- Wearing looser underwear
- Avoiding tight pants

After you've consulted your doctor and have a list of healthy steps to take, add pictures of them to your vision board. You could look for photos of healthy food, a bottle of folic acid, a woman taking regular walks outside and relaxing to reduce stress. The same is true for men–look for photos of things that can increase your fertility, including healthy behavior, less stress, and looser-fitting clothing, along with pictures of the baby to come. Remember to always find the positive side of the situation to reflect on your board, not the negative.

## Summary

- A vision board is a great tool for reminding you of the changes you need to make in order to reach your goal, whether that is losing weight, improving your endurance in a particular type of activity, or winning a sporting event.
- If your goal is to lose weight, you can use a vision board to show images of behaviors you need to adopt, such as taking the stairs instead of the elevator, eating more produce, and drinking more water.

- If you're battling an illness or a chronic disease, it can be tough to see too far into the future, but a vision board can help boost your spirits and remind you of the important people in your life.
- If you're a smoker trying to quit, find pictures of activities you'll be able to participate in once you're a nonsmoker, and include photos of people in your life you'll be able to spend more time with once your lungs heal.

Want a little help figuring out what to put on your healthy habits vision board? Use these questions to zero in on what images will help you become the healthier person you envision.

What are your healthiest habits?

_____

_____

_____

_____

What are some habits that are unhealthy?

_____

_____

_____

_____

Do you have lifestyle habits that you'd like to improve?

_____

_____

_____

_____

Are there any new habits you'd like to adopt?

_____

_____

_____

_____

What are some of the benefits you'd like to see from those changes?

_____

_____

_____

_____

# CHAPTER 16

# Your Spiritual Self

Sometimes, the one thing we really need in our lives isn't a person or a thing but a purpose. For many, this comes in the form of religious faith or spirituality. Believing in a higher power can help put our lives into perspective and push us to look outward, to see where we can make a difference in the world.

If you're feeling that there's more you could be doing to make the world a better place, you can use a vision board to find a role that is right for you. You might decide you need to spend more time studying religious texts, join a church congregation, or find a cause or a ministry you can be part of. Whether you have already decided what you need to do to fulfill your spiritual goals or you're in search of your purpose, you can use a vision board to guide you.

## Your Relationship to the World

Spirituality can be much more than going to church every Sunday. Your faith and your spirituality can consist of whatever connects you to the world and its inhabitants. That might mean volunteering with local, national, or international charities or events; taking a more active role in the leadership or management of your place of worship; or making a commitment to pray each day or before meals. Whatever action you want to take to feel more connected to your higher power is what your vision board should show.

### Reflecting Your Faith

So how, exactly, do you wish your life were different spiritually? That's the best question to ask yourself as you begin to design your vision board. If something spiritual is missing from your life, what do you need to do to feel closer to your higher power, your God, or your gods?

*A spiritual board is likely to show more community involvement than things and money.*

A good place to start is with your faith. Do you believe in God or a higher power? Whether you're an adherent of the Bahá'í Faith, a Buddhist, a Christian, or a Muslim, or you're part of a Wiccan or other spiritual group, there are things you can do to become more spiritually aware.

If you're feeling somewhat disconnected from your faith, how about outlining what you can do to play a bigger role in your faith community? That might include:

- Attending worship services
- Studying the Bible
- Volunteering at events
- Joining a choir or musical group
- Offering to teach Sunday school
- Volunteering for missionary work

- Participating in community outreach
- Volunteering for service work
- Nominating yourself for a leadership role

These are only a few of the possible ways you can become a more active member of your faith community or your congregation. If you feel called to help in a particular way, pursue how else you can apply your skills and talents. For example, you might volunteer to serve breakfast at a local soup kitchen once a month or attend church services at least three times a month. Or maybe your spirituality is more connected to the earth, so you could set a goal to spend a certain number of hours in nature or create a composting system at home to help the earth regenerate.

As you select ways to involve yourself more deeply in your faith, look for images showing similar activities to place on your vision board.

When creating a spiritual vision board, consider looking for words from scripture or religious teachings that speak to you and are meaningful. Print those out and glue them onto your board along with pictures.

## What Will You Do Differently?

Although becoming a more involved member of a faith community is one way to become more spiritual or to reflect your spirituality, you can connect with God or your higher power in more private ways. Some ways Christians, for example, can do this include:

- Praying during the day
- Saying grace before meals

- Attending church on Sunday
- Participating in Communion
- Refraining from using the word "God" in vain
- Showing respect for parents
- Granting forgiveness to others
- Being honest

There are many more ways to be a better Christian, with the Ten Commandments serving as the perfect guide, but even small actions, such as sharing or being kind to others, go a long way toward being a better member of a community. If your faith has a similar guide to behavior and worship, that guide would be a great place to turn to for ideas regarding your own actions.

After you identify the ways you'd like to change your behavior or involvement, look for images to add to your vision board that show these ways. You might have photos of people at worship, people volunteering at a soup kitchen, a Bat Mitzvah service, someone meditating outdoors, or someone reading quietly from a religious text.

When Oprah did a show on vision boards about ten years ago, Teresa Bondora thought it was "mysterious magic silliness." But when she heard tales of success from people on the show, she decided to make one. "I was in dire need, so I figured at the very least it would help me focus and put on paper exactly what I wanted, so I could tell myself and put it out there," she explains. When she found it the other day, she saw that everything she had put on her board years ago—the doting husband, new car, money to invest in the stock market, her own home, and weight loss—she had received.

CREATE YOUR VISION BOARD

# Faith-Based Work

Ministering to others through volunteer and missionary work is another way to express your spirituality. There are a number of ways to invest your time in faith-based work, which you can add to your vision board.

## Mission Participation

Some churches or congregations include missionary work as part of their faiths. Members of The Church of Jesus Christ of Latter-day Saints, for example, often spend two years during their early twenties away on missions preaching God's word. Other spiritual groups encourage missionary work in other countries.

If this is something that appeals to you, picture what the experience would be like and then seek photos and images that match that imagined experience. If there is a particular country or area you would like to visit and work in, make sure you identify it. If you'd like to go with a sibling or partner, make sure you include him or her, too, on your vision board.

## Volunteer Efforts

Even if missionary work isn't in your future, investing time in bettering your local community is another way to feel fulfilled and valued while also helping those who are less fortunate.

A good starting point for envisioning yourself doing volunteer work is to assess the types of organizations that interest you. Are there certain groups of people or social issues you'd most like to help? Examples of causes you could support include:

- Hunger
- Education
- Children's welfare
- Domestic violence
- Substance abuse
- Gun violence
- Bullying
- The environment
- Pets
- Peace
- Disease or health challenges

Generally, causes that have touched your life or your friends' or family's lives are a good fit, because you have an emotional connection. When you're emotionally invested in helping a particular segment of the population, such as newborns, teens, or married women in abusive relationships, you will contribute in a more substantial way. Or if your passion is to help improve the lives of the homeless, the hungry, or the illiterate, for example, you'll receive such satisfaction and fulfillment when you see that you can make a difference.

Kathleen Watson and her husband wanted to attend the Quest for Global Healing conference in Bali and stay for an extra two weeks afterward, but they didn't have the funds to afford the expensive trip. Sure, they could have charged it, but they preferred to find another way. Kathleen requested conference brochures and kept them sitting out where she could see them, and she surfed the web researching Bali, saving a number of Balinese websites as "favorites" so she could get back to them and imagine how wonderful a trip would be. Although she didn't glue the images to a formal vision board, she looked at them frequently, reminding herself of her goals, using the pictures just like a vision board. A short while later, as they debated whether to spring for the trip, they received two unsolicited offers to purchase land Kathleen had inherited in Florida. The twenty-five thousand dollars that changed hands provided more than enough for the conference and the vacation.

Volunteering can sometimes take on a life of its own, taking more time than you originally anticipated. To avoid this, you can set time limits or start by volunteering at a particular event, with clear start and end dates or times. That's a good way to see whether the work really resonates with you. You can reflect such time limits on your board using words and numbers, which will also help you identify when you've achieved an objective.

If volunteering is something you'd like to do more of, look for pictures that show people helping others, doing work similar to what you'd like to do. And just because you're not aware of opportunities to walk dogs, sort books, or cook meals for others yet, by putting those activities on your vision board, you will be very likely to attract just the right organization in need of your help.

Be careful about the images you use, however. Since your conscious mind can't distinguish between what you do and don't want, you wouldn't want to include pictures of hungry or homeless people on your board, lest you should attract that kind of lifestyle for yourself. Keep the focus on people who are helping, rather than on the people being helped.

## Participation in a Spiritual Community

Another way to become closer to God or another higher power is to participate more fully or actively in a spiritual community. If you don't have a place of worship where you feel comfortable, you can start by finding one. Seek out a congregation or group of like-minded people who make you feel welcome and appreciated as you worship.

### Contributions to a Place of Worship

In addition to connecting you with organizations in need of your support and assistance, your vision board can also lead you to a place of worship, if that is one of your goals. If you're on the hunt for a church, synagogue, mosque, or other spiritual home, use your vision board to clarify and feature pictures of what you'd like that place to be like. What would you like it to look like? How would you like to feel when you're there? What kinds of people would you like to meet and worship with? Now place pictures on your board to help you find that place.

Once you've found a spiritual home, you can be of service to the organization in many ways. Examples include volunteering during worship services, assisting in building upkeep and maintenance, and providing outreach to members of the church or temple who can't make it to services. Many roles need to be filled—it's just a matter of deciding which would be most satisfying for you.

Janis Ericson has used vision boards since she was a teenager, with great success. Several years ago, she created a board for a new business she was in the process of starting, along with pictures of places to which she wanted to travel—including Scotland, London, Virginia Beach, and San Francisco. Janis also included images of the amount of money she wanted to earn and the team she wanted to hire to help her realize the dream. Four years later, she now has the business she's always wanted, a home in the San Francisco Bay Area, and the opportunity to travel the world giving seminars.

Finding pictures of people doing good deeds inside a church, temple, or mosque might be a bit challenging, unless you can find some trade magazines for faith-based organizations. Instead, you can focus on the task you'd like to perform. If you know you'd be good at managing the organization's finances, put images of those types of activities on your board, perhaps next to a picture of your place of worship. Focus on what you'd like to do, and you will surely find opportunities to pursue that interest.

If your goal is to bless your church or faith-based organization with a monetary donation, make sure your vision board has pictures of money and your place of worship. You could even draw pictures of a collection plate and your donation in it.

## Role in Place of Worship

Another way to be of service to your faith is to take on a role within your congregation or at your place of worship. Beyond helping to maintain the facility in which you worship, could you take on responsibility for some aspect of the service? Maybe you want to join a committee devoted to addressing issues of importance to the faith community? Like most nonprofit organizations, most faith communities are in constant need of qualified people to serve as leaders in some capacity.

If you'd like to take on a more active role, your vision board should include pictures of you leading others as well as participating in the activities you see yourself helping with. You might look for some photos of a singer in choir robes or someone doing a reading from a church pulpit, for example.

## Summary

- If being more spiritually fulfilled is a goal, you can reflect that on your vision board in a number of ways. One is to use images of people doing the type of work you'd like to do, whether that's participating in an overseas mission, volunteering locally, or attending church more regularly.
- You can use your vision board to reflect your view of your own spirituality and the path you'd like to be on.

CREATE YOUR VISION BOARD

- Missionary work, or introducing others to your faith, is one way to participate in your faith-based organization's activities. Pictures of what you would do and where you would go should be front and center on your board.
- Another way to be more spiritual is to become more involved in your local community, to give back. Joining service organizations and efforts is another way to better yourself and those in need.

Want a little help figuring out what to put on your spirituality vision board? Use these questions to zero in on what will bring you closer to your higher power.

How do you define spirituality?

_____

_____

_____

_____

Do you consider yourself a spiritual person?

_____

_____

_____

_____

How is that spirituality reflected in your daily routine?

_____

_____

_____

_____

What could you do to become a more spiritual person?

_____

_____

_____

_____

How would those changes impact you and your lifestyle?

_____

_____

_____

_____

# PART 4

# How to Use a Vision Board

Okay, your vision board is complete, so now what? Creating a board is only part of the process of making progress toward your goals, and this part of the book will help you understand what to do, what not to do, and what other forms your boards can take. You also will learn how to keep your board updated and how to take it with you everywhere you go.

# CHAPTER 17

# Avoiding Common Pitfalls

Now that you've made a vision board and are devoting time to visualizing your many goals, you're probably wondering when success will come. How long will it take to manifest that new car or that trip to Scotland you've always wanted to take? The truth is, no one knows. How soon you manifest things on your board depends a lot on you and how you respond to opportunities that arise.

Mindset plays a big role. That is, a lot of things can get in the way of potential success, starting with attitude. If you began the process of creating a vision board with skepticism and doubt, you may never see those goals come to fruition. The less you believe you are capable and worthy of the things you want, the lower the odds are of those desires materializing.

Neurologists, physicists, physicians and more have studied how the brain functions and reported on what humans can do to make better use of it. The Law of Attraction holds that whatever you think about and focus on, you will bring into your life, and those who study the brain concur that, with effort, you can bring about physical changes in your brain. What you concentrate on can have a real impact on your reality.

If you believe that your vision board can work but are having trouble manifesting your goals, it's possible you've encountered one or more pitfalls associated with vision boards.

## Have You Hit a Roadblock?

If it's been quite a while since you prepared your vision board and you've been following my advice—looking at it regularly, imagining what it will feel like to achieve those goals and trusting that success will come—but don't feel you're making progress, it's time to take a step back. Is something in the way of your success?

### Your Expectations

Examining your expectations is a good first step. What did you honestly expect to happen after you created your vision board? Did you think that new multimillion-dollar recording contract would just drop in your lap, or the new Bentley you posted on your board would arrive on your doorstep with no strings attached? A vision board isn't magic, and it won't cause your dreams to come true instantly, but it will get you on the right path. While changes generally don't happen overnight, a vision can accelerate the pace at which they do materialize. Just be realistic.

If you're like some people, you may have figured that it couldn't hurt to create a vision board, but you might not have truly believed that it would do much good. The thing about expectations is that, as with the Law of Attraction, you usually get what you expect. Expect to make slow progress? You will. Expect to see little in the way of results? That's exactly what will happen. As Henry Ford said, "Whether you think you can or you think you can't, you're right." Set your sights low and you'll never make any significant headway toward your dreams.

So, if you're not expecting your vision board to manifest much, that's why it's not doing anything for you—you have no faith in the power of the universe to attract what you desire. That situation won't change until you start believing that what you posted on your vision board is your destiny.

## Explaining Failure

Sometimes, success seems elusive because other things keep getting in the way. Maybe you suddenly received a tax bill that ate up the money you had been setting aside for your new computer. Maybe your car suddenly died, or you got fired, or your boyfriend dumped you, or a number of other unattractive situations came up. You may perceive these situations as failures or as circumstances beyond your control that impeded your success. In fact, they may actually be unrecognized opportunities.

In many cases, what initially appears to be failure, such as not getting that new job you really wanted, turns out to be a major opportunity. In the case of the job, if you didn't get this one, a much better one is on the horizon. You only need to be patient and keep applying for other positions.

> Lisa Bell invited twenty friends over to a New Year's Eve party devoted to creating vision boards. Each partygoer was given a blank board, scissors, and glue, and everyone brought magazines to cut up and use. On Lisa's board, she posted pictures of a glorious new kitchen, complete with gleaming stainless-steel appliances. After all the guests had left, Lisa loaded her fifteen-year-old dishwasher, turned it on, and nothing happened. It was broken. Coincidence? She thinks not. So, of course, she headed out the next day to purchase a new stainless-steel dishwasher at a special New Year's Day sale—step one in manifesting her new kitchen.

Don't let setbacks become excuses that can quickly become bigger roadblocks to success. When you have a convenient reason why something didn't occur, it's easy to stop working toward it or to stop looking for a workaround.

Trust that things happen for a reason. When things don't go the way you expect, you may have to find a new path or redouble your efforts, and if you want something bad enough, you shouldn't have any trouble finding the inspiration or personal resolve to do it.

Another vision board "don't" is to sit back and wait for success to drop in your lap. It's not going to happen. Your vision board will bring opportunities to your consciousness, but you need to recognize them and pursue them. Success takes action.

# Fear

Besides excuses, fear also gets in the way of success with a vision board. Maybe you fear failure, so you don't even pursue what you really want. Or maybe you fear success and the additional responsibilities and challenges it will present. Either way, fear often manifests itself as self-sabotage, where you subconsciously ruin your chances for success. If you're not manifesting items on your vision board, fear could be at the root.

## Self-Sabotage

Self-sabotage occurs when you, typically unknowingly, ruin your chances of achieving some desired outcome. Maybe you go out partying the night before an exam or you present an offer on a house that is 40 percent below the asking price— far below the 10 percent average discount sellers expect to give. In both cases, you make conscious choices that may have an outcome that logic dictates you wouldn't generally want, such as performing poorly on the test and having your real estate offer rejected. However, other subconscious reasons may be impacting your logical mind.

So, although you may have pictures of a cruise to Greece or a new baby on your vision board, unless you are 100 percent sure you want those things, it's possible to sabotage your own efforts. In these examples you might schedule the trip during an important business conference and have to back out, or you might say you want another baby but then find many excuses not to try to conceive.

The only way to identify whether you're self-sabotaging your vision board goals is to honestly evaluate your goals and what's been happening to interfere with your success. Can you spot any actions you've taken, or even examples of inaction, that have hampered your success? Are you positive you still want the items you've placed on your board?

## Fear of Success

If you feel any twinge of doubt about a major goal—an accomplishment most people would value—perhaps you are afraid of what that success will mean for you or the changes it could bring.

When you imagine yourself having achieved your goals, what do you expect will change? Is there anything you'd like not to change? For example, with fame comes money, prestige, and fans—but it can also bring safety concerns, along with worries about how long your fifteen minutes of fame will last, what will come next, and where you'll need to live to make the most of it.

When you feel your body tense with anxiety or nerves regarding a particular goal, ask yourself, "What's the worst that can happen?" Whether you're nervous about reaching a goal or not reaching a goal, what is the worst that can happen, really? When you realize that the worst-case scenario probably isn't so bad after all, you may be able to forge ahead without fear.

With many opportunities come tradeoffs, and you need to feel comfortable that you can successfully deal with the coming changes. If you feel anxious about the next stage of your life after accomplishing one or more of the goals on your vision board, fear of success may be what's hampering your progress.

## Fear of Failure

Another thing that can hamper your ability to reach your goals is fear of failure. Sometimes, we worry so much about what could happen if we don't succeed that we do nothing and become stymied. Of course, doing nothing is a choice, too, that brings results of its own—sometimes good, sometimes bad.

If you are worried you won't ever achieve a goal on your vision board, your fear of failure may be preventing you from realizing success. To get past this, you have two options—take the photo off so you can work on other goals or come to grips with the fact that if you don't succeed, it's because there is something even better that is meant for you. Don't let fear be part of the equation.

# Doubt

Fear of failure is related to feelings of doubt and low self-confidence. When you don't truly believe you are capable of attaining a certain goal, you won't. It's as if you won't let yourself be successful.

## Self-Doubt

Overcoming self-doubt is critical for success with your vision board. Unfortunately, it's easier said than done, especially if you've doubted yourself for years.

To quiet the skeptic in you, don't write on your vision board in your own hand—have someone else do it or use a computer to print out words and phrases. When your brain sees your own handwriting, you may scoff internally and bring up those feelings of doubt and denial, but when you see someone else's handwriting, your brain is more willing to believe and accept what is written.

Try reflecting on the successes you've had in your life. Remember all of the times you tried to do something and succeeded. Compare yourself to others and realize that your skills and talent are superior to those of many around you, so why shouldn't you be successful in your dreams?!

Some people create journals or files of notes from other people telling them how great they are or complimenting them on their performance. When they start to doubt their abilities, they can get a boost by looking through those encouraging words. You may want to start one yourself, to remind yourself of your past successes and to prepare yourself for the future.

## Skeptics Around You

Quieting the skeptics and doubters around you—your family, friends, teammates, colleagues, neighbors, and so on—is actually much easier than quieting the doubter within you. When you recognize that the people you hang out with aren't aiming for the same levels of success as you, consider looking for some new people to spend time with.

Business philosopher Jim Rohn states that you are the average of the five people you surround yourself with most. So take a look at your five closest pals—are they at your same level or above, or are they below you in their goal setting? If they're below you, then they are unlikely to be your biggest supporters when it comes to your dreams and manifesting your vision board. Expect that they will be skeptical and continue on your own path to success.

## Refocus Your Energy

Creating your vision board is only the first step in achieving your goals. You've defined your goals, visualized them, and prepared a tool to help show you how to attain them, but you're not there yet. You need to use your vision board properly to bring about the changes in your life that you desire. Here are some important steps to take now to start generating some results from your vision board.

### Stay Focused

With or without a vision board, many people fail to bring their dreams to fruition because they lose focus as they get sidetracked or distracted by other goals that come up along the way. Sometimes they can find their way back, sometimes not.

After you hang your vision board on your wall, tack it up on a bulletin board, or place it within a binder or planner you carry with you, it's important that you look at it regularly. You must spend time visualizing yourself achieving the success you show on your board. You need to remind yourself of what it will feel like to earn that college degree, find your perfect mate, get that promotion you've been gunning for, or start that side business everyone's been encouraging you to open.

Sometimes, it takes more than focusing on the good to come to yield success with your vision board. Instead, think about the discomfort you may be feeling in certain areas of your life. Have you had enough yet? Are you ready to make some changes so you can get rid of that pain, whether physical or mental? If so, what action will you commit to right now to get started?

For your vision board to work, you need to reflect on it daily. Don't just put it up and forget about it. If you do, it won't work, because you won't be engaging your brain to figure out how you'll achieve the success you want.

## Upgrade Your Circle of Friends

Although you don't have to ditch every person who isn't a complete supporter of your dream, it certainly couldn't hurt to start traveling in new circles and meeting new people. If many of your vision board goals are career-related, how about joining a new trade or business association and attending those meetings? If you're working on a college degree, how about spending more time in class or the library than with your buddies doing nothing in the dorm? Or if you're working toward starting your own business, think about where supporters would be and go there—the Small Business Development Center in your area, the Small Business Administration, and the Service Corps of Retired Executives are all great groups to tap into.

Think about where successful people with similar dreams and goals would be spending time and go there. Being amongst them will likely inspire you and may even provide you with unexpected opportunities.

## Practice Creative Visualization

Sometimes, lack of progress in manifesting items on your vision board is due to a lack of focus on your part. Spending time looking at your vision board, imagining what your success will feel like, and considering the many ways you could reach those goals is important. One technique that you'll want to be sure you're using is creative visualization.

Essentially, creative visualization is closing your eyes and picturing yourself achieving a goal. It's a mini movie of you doing what you've been working toward. Olympic athletes use creative visualization frequently, picturing themselves at the race, in the pool, or schussing down the ski slope to a win. The more they play their own movies in their heads, the more prepared they are to win. That's what you need to do to prepare yourself for the success you seek.

Be aware that what you put on your vision board may manifest itself in ways that you don't exactly expect. Years ago, Sandra of Pittsburgh created a vision board to meet a mate. She included on it a cartoon drawing of Albert Einstein, a picture of a box of chocolates, something about incredible sex, and a beautiful girly teapot with "Tea for two" written under it. In response, her vision board presented her with a nuclear scientist with the sex drive of a rabbit who wore a girly kimono on weekends when he cooked. Unfortunately, the relationship didn't last long. And to ensure that the universe understood it was not a good match, Sandra burned her vision board with intent.

## Stay Enthusiastic

Although you may hope for overnight success, a vision board is designed to help show you the way over the long haul, which is likely to be more than twenty-four hours. It's your vision of your future, which may be next week or several years ahead. You don't really know when you'll reach your goals, but it's important to stay motivated and optimistic along the way.

As you look at your vision board, remind yourself what it will feel like to achieve your dream. Experience the joy, the satisfaction, and the triumph of having reached your goal.

It's important to feel these sensations each time you look at your vision board. Any doubts or negative self-talk needs to be squelched—work hard not to let yourself even consider the possibility that you won't succeed. You will be successful; it's just a matter of time.

Scott Mooney is an illustrator-turned-life coach and a healer whose illustration contracts a few years ago were typically worth 150 to 300 dollars each. To increase their value, he created a vision board and took a picture of a hundred-dollar bill, added an extra zero in Photoshop to make it a thousand-dollar bill, and placed three together on the board. He meditated in front of the board each morning, and within a couple of days, he landed two illustration jobs for three hundred dollars each. "But why not three thousand dollars each?" he wondered. Then he realized that each time he looked at the made-up thousand-dollar bills, he automatically saw hundreds instead. After finding and placing more realistic thousand-dollar bills on the board, he landed a three thousand-dollar gig. After adding more money to the board, Scott landed more and more valuable jobs.

## Summary

- The act of creating a vision board is not enough to yield success. You also need to reflect on it, look at it, and imagine yourself as having already achieved the goals shown on the board.
- Imagining the feeling of having attained your goals, whatever they are, will help your brain determine the best path to getting that feeling in real life.
- Success with your vision board takes belief and confidence. Knowing you are worthy of success is half the battle in achieving it.
- Don't allow yourself to start questioning your progress, your goals, or your abilities. Cut yourself off from others who don't believe in your success, too.
- Even when it may not feel as if you are making progress toward success, you are. Watch for new opportunities that may appear unexpectedly— they're a sign of your progress.
- If your goals have changed or you've started to doubt whether vision boards work, you've sabotaged yourself. Get back on track by recommitting yourself to achieving your goals.

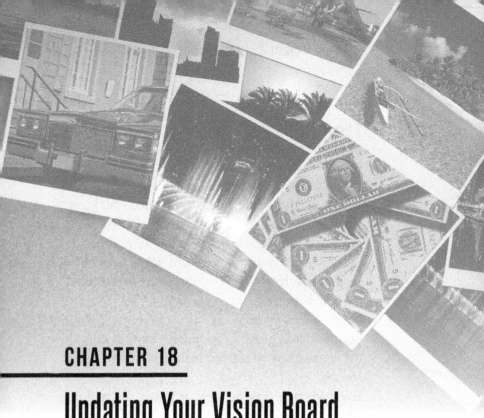

# CHAPTER 18

# Updating Your Vision Board

The great thing about a vision board is that it's a snapshot of where you are today and where you're headed. Your current goals, wants, and aspirations are all captured on your vision board, based on where you are right now. As soon as something in your life changes, though, your view of the future and your goals change. Your vision board should change, too, to reflect your new focus and status.

As you achieve certain milestones and make progress in various areas of your life, you'll want to note those things on your vision board. That means removing or crossing off goals you've met or resetting other goals so that you're constantly bettering yourself and your situation.

## Keeping Your Board Current

In order to keep your vision board current, you need to look at it and reflect on it daily. Where are you with respect to the items on your board? Are you close to attaining any of them? Have you already accomplished some and moved on to other goals since creating it?

### Update Your Goals

As noted, you should update your vision board as you reach certain milestones or achieve individual goals. That means either adding new goals or stepping up your current performance to the next level. To do this, you can peel the picture or phrase off, cover it up with a new and bigger goal, or check or cross it off with a marker—something to note that you're no longer pursuing that goal.

If your goal was to shoot an eighty in a round of golf and you did that, you might set a new goal of shooting a seventy-five. Or if you wanted to achieve a 3.4 grade point average in school and you did that, maybe next semester's goal is to reach 3.5 or 3.6.

Some people start the new year with a new vision board— new goals for the next 365 days. If you like this idea, you may even want to host a New Year's Eve party devoted to guests creating their own vision boards.

Sometimes, you may just outgrow a goal, in which case you'll want to take it off or replace it with your new goal. This is often the case with material things, such as cars, jewelry, and clothing. As fashions change or a new, trendier product is released, old "wants" fade away. If they're no longer important or relevant to you, they shouldn't appear on your board.

## Signs of Progress

Every day you're getting closer to realizing your dreams, although in many cases you're not aware of it. You may not recognize that the person you just met at the gym will help you find the angel investor you've been looking for, or you may not yet see that your decision to start buying organic foods will result in stunning physical changes.

Have changes, even minor, been occurring in your life? Have you been presented with new challenges and opportunities? Have you been meeting new people? Have you been required to make decisions that will impact the course of your career or life?

Maybe the green card you've been waiting for finally came through, for example, or you just heard that you earned a place in your town's juried art show. Milestones like these confirm that you're headed in the right direction, and you should make sure your vision board reflects your latest situation.

If partial attainment of a goal comes through, you may find you need to update what's on your board. For example, if you are approved for a mortgage—one of your featured goals—but it's more than or less than what you had expected, the dream home you have on your board may need to change to match. Or if you lose ten of the twenty pounds you were shooting for, you may decide you're happy with your current weight, or you may find you're inspired to try to lose a total of thirty pounds.

Some vision board users find that transferring things they've obtained or achieved to a separate board—an achievement or success board—helps remind them of how far they've come. You could also call it a gratitude board—a board that reflects what you've accomplished or received for which you are truly thankful.

Any or all of these situations suggest that change is occurring. It may be minor, such as the chance to have your home painted at a discount, or it could be major, such as being offered a new job. Both, however, could spell movement toward your goals (maybe having your house freshly painted will boost its value overnight and help you sell it faster when you spot your dream home sixty days from now).

Sometimes, vision boards have "surprising twists," says Alaia Leighland, who has used vision boards for years. When she wanted a Mitsubishi SUV a few years ago, she drew it on her board herself but didn't happen to have the color pen she really wanted in order to match the color of the car she hoped to manifest, so she used what she had available. It turns out the SUV she manifested was the color of the pen she ended up using.

After you accomplish a goal, either check it off or remove it altogether and replace it with a new goal.

> A couple of years ago, Latoicha Givens and her girlfriends decided to do something different around New Year's. They created vision boards to show what they wanted to accomplish in the next twelve months. On Latoicha's board was an Acura MDX Touring Edition, a new home in a particular neighborhood, and travel to Europe. Within one month, she and her husband purchased the Acura MDX, and the exact house she wanted was put back on the market for a hundred twenty-five thousand dollars less than before. They're currently trying to buy it.

# Outgrowing Some Goals

No matter what age you are, it's a given that your goals will change over time. Whether you're sixteen or sixty-one, what you want will shift as your environment and situation change. At sixteen, you may be most worried about getting good grades, being accepted into a good college, earning your driver's license, and looking pretty for the boys in your school. At sixty-one, you may be more concerned with retiring while you're healthy, caring for an aging parent, finding time for yourself, and staying in shape. You and your goals change over time.

## Your Goals Will Change

While your major goals probably won't change every week or every month, they may change every year. As your skills, interests, financial well-being, health, and romantic status shift, so too will your dreams. That's to be expected. As people and situations around you change, what you want for yourself and your family will change.

Take another look at your vision board. Is everything on it still meaningful to you? Have you already achieved some of the goals? Do you have new, more important ones that should be on it? Make sure the pictures and messages your vision board contains are what you're still aiming for. If not, you need to get back in sync.

Whereas last year you might have been fighting for a promotion, this year you may simply be aiming to hold on to your job until the recession turns around. Or if your concern last year was with your daughter's making the cheerleading squad, now that she's made it, you may be thinking ahead to getting the team to nationals. Every step you take, whether ahead or back, impacts where you go next. And that, in turn, affects what your vision board looks like.

## Do You Feel Stressed?

Your vision board should be a source of joy, direction, and comfort to you as it helps you visualize where you're headed. It should reduce the stress you may feel about your future by showing you what it will look like.

If you're feeling pressured or uncomfortable about your future or your board, there is something on it that is not a true goal—something that does not resonate with you. Maybe it's a picture of a goal your parents have always had for you, so you felt compelled to include it, despite the fact that it is of no interest to you. Or maybe you have a goal on there that was once so important but now, as you've come to understand yourself better, is really no longer applicable.

Any signs of goals or dreams that are not truly your goals will cause you stress. They will interfere with your progress, too. So, if you're wondering whether you're getting anywhere with your vision board, reconfirm that what you're working toward is still relevant and true for you. If anything on your board no longer feels right, take it off right away.

Sometimes, the key to finding what is tripping you up or slowing you down is looking at where you feel out of balance. Is there a part of your life that feels like it is dominating everything else? Is there a problem that is overshadowing your progress? If one thing dominates your thoughts or your actions, that's likely the source of your slow progress. See if you can resolve or change the situation for your benefit.

## Stretching for Bigger Goals

After you accomplish certain dreams or reach specific milestones you've set for yourself, you may decide it's time to shift your attention elsewhere. That's fine. But another option is to look for the next rung on the ladder—you've moved a step ahead, so what's after that? Setting new, higher goals makes a lot of sense and can result in even greater long-term success, because you'll be sticking with one strength and building on it.

## Postponing or Putting Off Others

Although it would be wonderful if you knew that you'd achieve every single goal you placed on your vision board, the reality is that some goals simply won't come to fruition. Those goals are typically the ones that you really weren't all that excited about anyway, so you didn't invest much energy in pursuing them.

But you may consciously decide you need to back off of certain goals or targets. Rather than ignoring or overlooking some of your goals, you do have the option to decide "not now," or "not anymore." If you do, you'll free up energy to invest in goals you've decided are more important right now.

When you elect to redirect that energy, you'll want to remove those goals and set them aside. Take them off your board completely, so there is no mistaking that you shouldn't be working on how to achieve them. They're no longer important.

## Success!

Of course, a better, more enjoyable reason to remove items from your vision board is that you've succeeded in manifesting them. You did it!

### Removing Images

The easiest way to indicate that a goal has been achieved is to remove the image or words related to it. Just peel or tear the item off. As mentioned, some people like tracking their progress and might suggest that you relocate the images, rather than tossing them, but that's up to you.

Other vision board users note that a goal has been achieved by checking or "x-ing" out images of goals that have been realized. If noting that a goal has been completed gives you encouragement and energy, then feel free to cross out the photo and continue on with the same board, focusing now on the unchecked images.

Jean Newell, the inventor of the personal utility pouch, or PUP, which holds the many electronic devices we carry with us, is a firm believer in visualization. On her vision board is the QVC logo, which led to her demonstrating her product on the QVC channel and selling 1.5 million dollars of her PUP bags during thirty-five appearances in eighteen months. Her two references to Donny Deutsch and his show *The Big Idea* on her board led to two appearances. And her Photoshopped picture of herself with *Today Show* anchor Matt Lauer became reality when she was interviewed by Matt. There are many other TV shows she aspires to be a guest on and which she has on her vision board.

## Look Ahead

As you cross certain goals off your to-do list, don't just smile and move on. Stop and reflect on what you did right. What got you this far? What made the difference and enabled you to achieve your goal? Did you learn a new skill? Meet someone who acted as a liaison to get you a coveted introduction? Spend some free time daydreaming, during which you found inspiration? Did one event lead you to your goal, or was it a series of events? How can you replicate your past thoughts and actions to yield a continuous stream of successes?

# Make Almost Any Space Work

It's a bit more difficult to find a space for a board you've already created, especially if it's oversized. Instead, consider starting with a board sized for a particular wall or designed to be placed in a certain spot. That way you won't encounter problems when it's ready to be displayed.

If you start to think about exactly where your vision board is going to go before you create it, you have the luxury of being able to cut your board to fit the space you have available. Don't select a twenty-by-twenty-four-inch board, for example, if your studio apartment wasn't designed to showcase such large works. Instead, cut the board down to ten by twelve inches and then glue your components on.

Another alternative, of course, is cutting down your board after you've made it, but you risk cutting off important photos around the edges.

Don't feel you have to hang the vision board, however. You don't. Simply look for an open spot where you can lean it against a wall, such as within a bookcase, on a shelf, or even on a small table. Just make sure it's visible.

## Summary

- The easiest way to keep your board current is to note when certain goals have been met. When that occurs, either remove the manifested images or cross them off, as you would an item on a checklist.
- If you like to track your successes, when you remove an item from your vision board, transfer it to a gratitude board or success board to see how far you've come.
- Another solution is to create new vision boards regularly. Some people create vision boards annually, and others create multiple boards—one for each area of their lives.

- As you update, remove, and replace images and goals attained, reflect on what you did to make each one happen. After you recognize the steps you took, make sure you try to replicate them to achieve even greater success going forward.

# CHAPTER 19

# Making an Always-Accessible Board

Although some experts might argue that the tactile act of cutting and pasting images to a board helps make the vision of the future more real, virtual cutting and pasting does have its advantages. Namely, you can quickly and easily move pictures around and add text and even music to bring your goals to life.

By uploading to your computer images you've gathered of yourself, friends, family, places you've traveled to, or material possessions you'd like to have, you can then merge them with stock images, inspirational quotes and phrases, and music to create a professional-looking montage. As your goals change, you can also quickly and easily update your online board without having to cut and paste a single picture using scissors and glue.

## Virtual Vision Boards Up Close and Personal

As Americans spend an increasing amount of time in front of a computer screen, whether to communicate via email, keep in touch with friends through social networking sites such as Facebook and Twitter, research plane tickets for an upcoming trip, or write a letter or memo, they are becoming ever more reliant on computers. Not only is the computer a research and communication tool, but it has also become a repository for important personal data—photos, videos, recipes, and stock portfolios can all be managed online rather than on paper. So, it makes perfect sense that a virtual vision board is the natural next step for many people.

Elise Touchette put together her first vision board with friends a few years ago. When she took a step back to consider her life goals—what she really wanted—she realized she wanted to be a backup singer. One of her friends, who was also preparing a vision board that night, is married to a drummer in a band. Later, when the friend mentioned to her husband that Elise had a picture of a backup singer on her vision board, he emailed Elise to see if she might want to perform with the band. A couple of weeks later, she was onstage singing with them for a twelve-song set—certainly the first of many future gigs if that's what Elise decides she wants.

## Computer-Generated Vision Boards

Although you can see your online vision board on a computer monitor, tablet, or smartphone (unless you print it out, of course), the process required to prepare it mirrors that of a physical board. In both cases, you contemplate your priorities and set goals, gather images that reflect the life you aim to create for yourself, couple them with inspiring quotes and sayings, place the components on a board of some type, and then place it somewhere you will regularly see it and reflect on it.

*Designing and constructing a vision board online can
be fairly fast and easy, since all the images and quotes
have already been compiled in one place for you.*

The biggest benefit of a virtual vision board is that it can be portable. If you download vision board software and create a board on a specific computer, you'll be able to pull your vision board up on the computer where the software resides. You can also save it to another computer, such as a laptop, if you're traveling.

If you subscribe to a vision board–building website, at a cost of less than ten dollars a month, you will be able to immediately pull up your latest and greatest board on an electronic device—computer, phone, or personal digital assistant equipped with an LCD screen and a wireless or cable internet connection.

Another option is to create an inspirational computer screen saver that runs whenever you're not actively using your computer. Use Google to find instructions for creating a custom screensaver for your particular operating system.

Although you will be viewing your vision board on a screen, rather than on a wall or bulletin board, it will look much the same, and it will work the same way.

All of the components of online vision boards are the same as the paper-based variety, although video and music can be incorporated online, too.

## Choosing Your Virtual Board Provider

You can go two ways when selecting a virtual vision board program. You can subscribe to a service that grants you continuous online access, or you can buy a software package outright.

Here are some websites where you can create vision boards through an online subscription:

- catalogofdreams.com
- visionboardsite.blogspot.com

The one big disadvantage of a software package is that you will be limited to the images and quotes available via download. You generally won't receive new images as they are added or be able to take advantage of new features—it's a fixed program, unless you buy the upgrade if and when it's offered.

# How They Work

Online vision boards are fairly simple to use, especially if you're computer savvy. Essentially, if you can open up a new document and move things around on-screen, you're halfway there.

## Images at the Ready

Vision board services and software all come with stock images and quotes and phrases that you can use to create your board. The stock photos are great to help you get started, but don't forget about using your own images. In fact, those can be far more powerful than a beautiful, professional stock photo in keeping you goal-focused.

You should have little trouble finding photos that reflect your goals and dreams in online vision board programs.

Use provided stock images when they make sense, but if there are images that you want to incorporate from photos you or a friend have taken, go for it. Most programs permit you to scan or upload images from other sources in addition to using those preloaded into the system. If the software does not permit you to upload your own, you may want to steer clear—that will severely limit your creativity and flexibility.

## Templates Are Tops

Another great tool you'll find with most vision board software programs is a library of templates to use.

A vision board template is a blank predesigned electronic vision board into which you can insert your chosen images and words. It's like a blank canvas that has been preformatted for easier electronic image placement. You choose the template design you prefer and then start adding in your pictures and phrases.

Except for graphic designers and artists who have been trained in visual presentation, it can be downright overwhelming to have to figure out where to place all the images you've gathered to make it pleasing to the eye. Done incorrectly, a vision board can appear cluttered and messy. Templates help eliminate the "explosion of photos" look by providing a structure into which you can place the images you've gathered. It's like a paint-by-numbers canvas.

## Reviewing Your Work

After you've chosen, uploaded, and placed your photos, images, and phrases, it's time to take a look at your first draft and decide if changes are needed. When working with a physical vision board, you might lay all your elements out first, shift them as necessary, and then glue them down. With an electronic vision board, you'll do the same, without the gluing. You can move images in seconds with the help of a mouse or stylus, even after you've saved their current locations. You can also add images later or take some off. That's the ultimate in flexibility that electronic vision boards offer.

Even after you've carefully placed each and every image, you can move them around or remove them later with ease, such as when you've achieved a particular goal.

# Online Pros and Cons

Online vision boards are very easy to use and can make the process quick and painless. Like paper-based boards, however, they, too, have their limitations, which you'll want to investigate before investing time in creating one.

## The Web Is the Place to Be

The biggest benefit of a virtual board is the speed with which you can prepare your board. Even if you decide to upload and feature your own images, preparing an electronic vision board is still faster than cutting, designing, and pasting pictures to a foam core board.

That advantage multiplies if you decide to create more than one board, such as a career board, a health board, and a romantic partner board. Access to online photos and a template to guide you make it a snap.

In addition, after you create your online board, you can go back and update it, move images around, add new ones, and delete old ones in minutes—maybe even seconds. Keeping your goals and dreams current without a hassle is a big plus.

The fact that you can access online vision boards from anywhere is another advantage. When you're daydreaming at work, you can't see the beautiful vision board you have hanging on your bedroom wall, but with an online board, you can simply pull it up on-screen or make it your screen saver. (Just don't let your boss see that one of your goals is to get a better-paying job ASAP.)

David Slocombe's home sits high on a hill and draws its water from a well. Before the well was dug, however, David used a vision board to keep the costs of drilling to a minimum. He started by spraying the number 179 on the spot where the well was to be dug and drew a picture of the truck digging the well to place on his vision board, along with gratitude statements and the total he wanted his bill to be. Once the digging process started, David spoke down the hole as it was being dug and thanked it for providing an abundance of water at 179 feet. Five weeks later, the crew hit water at 178 feet. Since his neighbors had to dig more than 260 feet for their wells, at forty dollars per foot, David feels very blessed.

## Tangible Is Tantamount

Of course, although ease of use and access are big benefits, there are also some disadvantages of virtual vision boards. The first is the cost. When you've finished creating a paper vision board, there are no more costs—you've bought the board, the images, and any glue you needed, and now you just need to hang it up. However, most online vision board software programs require a monthly subscription to access the board and update it. Although some have a free trial period, when that's up you'll pay five to ten dollars a month to be able to continue to access the board you've spent time creating. Another option, as mentioned, is to buy software outright, which can run forty dollars to sixty dollars. Either way, the costs add up, and within a month or two will exceed the cost of the paper board.

Even if you plunk down the cash for a software package, the one-time cost will still exceed the raw material costs for a paper board for many, many months. Make sure the convenience is worth it (and it may be).

Another downside of an electronic vision board is that the medium prevents you from getting up close and personal with the paper, photos, and glue. There is no tactile or kinesthetic involvement with your dreams, which can make them seem ethereal or beyond your reach. It's important that you believe that your goals are within your reach. With a paper board you can actually reach out and touch them, but with a virtual board, you can't.

Electronic vision boards also have some design constraints. Whereas you can control how cluttered or uncluttered your physical vision board is, many vision board programs come preloaded with background images and formats that end up making the result look a lot busier than a traditional board. That's not to say it won't work, just that it is formatted differently by virtue of the software program, and you should be aware of that before plunking down your credit card.

Finally, an online or computer-based vision board is great as long as you have access to a computer. When you don't, that vision board is out of view. If you can access your computer via a smartphone with a decent screen, this may not be an issue, or if you are always on the computer, you'll be able to look at your vision board frequently. If not, you may lose touch with those visions while your computer is turned off.

## Achieving Portability

It's easier to stay on track when you are constantly reminded of the goals and targets you've placed on your vision board. Like stepping on a bathroom scale each morning to check your weight, attention given to your vision board pays off by helping you shift course as needed or reinforcing your commitment to your future life. Given the positive impact of regularly looking at the goals you've posted on your vision board, imagine how much more quickly you'll achieve those goals if you could bring them with you wherever you go. A portable vision board could be just what you need to make progress.

After you've spent a fair amount of time crafting a rather large vision board that you can spot from across the room, the idea of shrinking it down to something that you can carry with you may not be appealing initially. But reducing its size is actually easier than you might imagine. Here are a few ideas:

- Make a mini you
- Carry the board in a binder
- Hang the board from a keychain

Just like Mini-Me in the *Austin Powers* movies, a scaled-down version of your vision board should contain everything you have on your full-size board, just in a smaller format.

One of the easiest ways to do this is to take your board to a copy shop and scan or photocopy it using the reduce function, so you can get it to fit on an 8.5-by-11-inch sheet of paper. Be sure to use a color copier to get the full effect. Then glue the copy onto a smaller foam core board or fold it so you can compact it further.

After you scan your vision board or photograph it, store a copy on a small flash or thumb drive, which you can take anywhere you go. That's the ultimate in portability. Simply plug your thumb drive into a computer at work or school, and your vision board will pop up.

If you're frequently on the go, another solution is to reduce your larger board to an 8.5-by-11-inch sheet of paper, use a three-hole puncher to punch holes in it, and then place it in a binder or daily planner. Enclosed within a binder, your vision board will be protected and private but easily accessible when you get bored in a meeting or are in a cab going across town.

Another option is to choose one goal—perhaps your primary objective at the moment—and feature that in a small frame or block hanging from your keychain.

Look for a small, clear acrylic frame attached to a hook for a keychain and insert your mini vision board for your main goal. For example, if it's a new job, you could type up a short description in the form of a help wanted ad and place it on one side of the frame, with a picture of you in your new office or company car.

*Although you can't fit your whole vision board in a one-by-one-inch frame, you can feature your biggest goal.*

# Jack Canfield's Goal Book

You can transform your wall-mounted vision board into a portable board or document in many ways. One way that bestselling author Jack Canfield recommends is to create a goal book containing all of the life goals you currently have for yourself. Store it in a three-ring binder or photo album; then you can pull out your goal book and reflect on your dreams and goals, as well as easily update it when those goals change—for instance, removing a goal when you've attained it.

## Your Materials

To make a goal book, find a three-ring binder or an empty photo album and paper. Your goal book should reflect all that you want for yourself and your family, just like a vision board. Now gather pictures of what you envision for yourself.

## Creating Your Goal Book

While a vision board features many photos and words in a collage, a goal book is a tad more organized. On each sheet of paper or page of your photo album, place one of your goals. If you hope to be married, you may show a photo of a set of wedding rings or a wedding gown you love and look forward to wearing. Then flip to the next page to show images of another of your goals, and so on.

As you find additional pictures that clarify your goals, feel free to add them to the appropriate pages. Take care not to let the book get cluttered. Your goal book should be like a catalog of your dreams and desires.

Entrepreneur Dana Abramson had long admired a local billionaire's business acumen, even hanging his photo on her wall as inspiration. Her goal was to meet him to discuss her business plan, hoping he might invest in it. But after several failed attempts to reach him, she lamented to a colleague that the only way she'd ever get to meet with him face-to-face was if she bumped into him somewhere. The next day, the newspaper announced he would be speaking at a local event. Recognizing the huge opportunity she had been given, Dana registered and approached him at the event. That bold introduction netted her a meeting and a mentor.

## Summary

- Creating an electronic vision board requires some kind of computing device, so you can either run downloaded software or log into a subscription service. Paying a fee for use will give you access to photos, words, and sometimes music you can use to construct your board.
- One of the major benefits of an online vision board is that it is much easier to modify than a board constructed with paper and glue.
- Some experts suggest that the act of reviewing, cutting, and pasting images and words can help connect you to your dreams and visions in a powerful way. That tactile connection is lost when you create a vision board online.
- One way to make your vision board is portable is to reduce its size. Take your wall-hung vision

board to a copy shop and reduce it on a copier or scan it and then print it out on smaller paper.

- Bestselling author Jack Canfield recommends using a goal book, which is essentially a vision board in portable form. Instead of arranging images and words on a board to be displayed, paste them on individual pages—one page per goal—and protect them in a three-ring binder or photo album.

# APPENDIX

## Resources

To learn more about the science behind vision boards, check into some of these helpful resources:

Allen, James. *As a Man Thinketh*. New York: Street & Smith, 1902.

Assaraf, John. *The Complete Vision Board Kit: Using the Power of Intention and Visualization to Achieve Your Dreams*. New York: Atria Books/Beyond Words, 2008.

Atkinson, William Walker. *Thought Vibration: The Law of Attraction in the Thought World*. Vista, CA: Boomer Books, 2008.

Canfield, Jack, and Mark Victor Hansen. *The Aladdin Factor.* New York: Berkley, 1995.

Canfield, Jack, and Mark Victor Hansen. *Dare to Win.* New York: Berkley, 1994.

Canfield, Jack, Mark Victor Hansen, and Les Hewitt. *The Power of Focus: How to Hit Your Business, Personal and Financial Targets with Absolute Certainty.* Deerfield Beach, FL: Health Communications, 2000.

Chopra, Deepak. *The Seven Spiritual Laws of Success: A Practical Guide to the Fulfillment of Your Dreams.* San Rafael, CA: Amber-Allen, 1994.

Cross, Lucinda. *Activate Your Vision Board: Learn how to Set Goals, Take Action & Get Your Vision off the Board and into Your Life in 40 Days or Less.* Corporate Mom Dropouts, 2015.

Dooley, Mike. *Manifesting Change: It Couldn't Be Easier.* New York: Atria Books, 2011.

Dyer, Wayne. *The Power of Intention.* Carlsbad, CA: Hay House, 2004.

Dyer, Wayne. *Wishes Fulfilled: Mastering the Art of Manifesting.* Carlsbad, CA: Hay House, 2013.

Fitzpatrick, Bill. *Master Success: Create a Life of Purpose, Passion, Peace and Prosperity.* Natick, MA: American Success Institute, 2000.

Gawain, Shakti, and Marci Shimoff. *Creative Visualization: Use the Power of Your Imagination to Create What You Want in Your Life.* Novato, CA: New World Library, 2016.

Grout, Pam. *E-Cubed: Nine More Energy Experiments That Prove Manifesting Magic and Miracles is Your Full-Time Gig.* London: Hay House, 2014.

Grout, Pam. *E-Squared: Nine Do-It-Yourself Energy Experiments That Prove Your Thoughts Create Reality.* London: Hay House, 2013.

Hicks, Esther, and Jerry Hicks. *The Law of Attraction: The Basics of the Teachings of Abraham.* Carlsbad, CA: Hay House, 2006.

Hill, Napoleon, and Dale Carnegie. *The Law of Success in Sixteen Lessons.* Meriden, CT: The Ralston Society, 1928.

Hill, Napoleon, and W. Clement Stone. *Success through a Positive Mental Attitude.* Englewood Cliffs, NJ: Prentice-Hall, 1977.

Hill, Napoleon. *Think and Grow Rich; Teaching, for the First Time, the Famous Andrew Carnegie Formula for Money-Making, Based upon the Thirteen Proven Steps to Riches.* Meriden, CT: The Ralston Society, 1937.

Kane, Christine. *The Complete Guide to Vision Boards: The Ultimate Starter Kit To Get Wildly Clear and Create the Life of Your Dreams.* Seattle, WA: Amazon Digital Services, 2016.

Katie, Byron, and Stephen Mitchell. *Loving What Is: Four Questions that Can Change Your Life.* New York: Harmony Books, 2002.

Kimbrow, Dennis P., Ph.D. *What Makes the Great Great: Strategies for Extraordinary Achievement.* New York: Doubleday, 1997.

Losier, Michael J. *Law of Attraction: The Science of Attracting More of What You Want and Less of What You Don't.* New York: Grand Central, 2010.

MacLelland, Bruce. *Prosperity Through Thought Force.* Elizabeth Towne, ed. New Delhi: Indigo Books, 2008.

McGraw, Phillip C., Ph.D. *Life Strategies: Doing What Works, Doing What Matters.* New York: Hyperion, 1999.

Miller, Sonia M. *The Attraction Distraction: Why the Law of Attraction Isn't Working for You and How to Get Results[md] FINALLY!* Long Island City: Alma Publishing, Inc., 2008.

Murphy, Joseph. *The Power of Your Subconscious Mind.* Floyd, VA: Wilder Publications, 2008.

Orman, Suze. *The Courage to Be Rich: Creating a Life of Material and Spiritual Abundance.* New York: Riverhead Books, 1999.

Peale, Norman Vincent. *The Power of Positive Thinking.* New York: Fireside, 2008.

Ponder, Catherine. *The Dynamic Laws of Prosperity.* New York: DeVorss, 1985.

Ray, James A. *The Science of Success: How to Attract Prosperity and Create Life Balance through Proven Principles.* La Jolla, CA: SunArk Press, 1999.

Robey, Dan. *The Power of Positive Habits.* Miami, FL: Abritt Publishing Group, 2003.

Samuels, Michael. *Just Ask the Universe: A No-Nonsense Guide to Manifesting your Dreams.* Self-published, 2011.

Schwarz, Joyce. *The Vision Board: The Secret to an Extraordinary Life.* New York: Harper Collins, 2008.

Shinn, Florence Scovel. *The Secret Door to Success.* Self-published, 1940.

Shinn, Florence Scovel. *The Game of Life and How to Play it.* Self-published, 1925.

Shinn, Florence Scovel. *Your Word Is Your Wand.* Self-published, 1928.

Smith, Hyrum W. *The 10 Natural Laws of Successful Time and Life Management: Proven Strategies for Increased*

*Productivity and Inner Peace.* New York: Warner Books, 1994.

Stanley, Thomas J., and William D. Danko. *The Millionaire Next Door.* New York: Pocket Books, 1996.

Stevens Annabelle, and Eiver Stevens. *How to Create and Use a Vision Board for Inspiration: Basics for Beginners.* Eternal Spiral Books, 2016.

Stone, W. Clement. *The Success System that Never Fails.* Englewood Cliffs, NJ: Prentice-Hall, 1962.

Wattles, Wallace D. *The Science of Getting Rich.* Elizabeth Towne Company, 1910.

Zander, Rosamund Stone, and Benjamin Zander. *The Art of Possibility: Transforming Personal and Professional Life.* New York: Penguin, 2000.

Zufelt, Jack M. *The DNA of Success: Know What You Want [el] To Get What You Want.* New York: Regan Books, 2002.

## Websites

www.abraham-hicks.com
www.applythelawofattraction.com
www.dreamitalive.com
www.thelawofattraction.com
www.therealsecretofsuccess.com
www.makeavisionboard.com

## Apps

Bloom app (App Store)
DreamCloud app (App Store)
Hay House Vision Board App (App Store and Google Play)

# ACKNOWLEDGMENTS

This project all began thanks to Rochester, New York, artist Joanne Sharpe, who had the foresight to offer a fun class in preparing vision boards a few years ago. After an evening creating my own, I was inspired to learn more so I could teach others. That led to many hours of study, practice, and, ultimately, to a book proposal.

Thank you to Debra Englander, editor extraordinaire, who connected me with Post Hill Press and helped bring this book to fruition. Thanks also to JT Coupal for his research skills and to all my writing friends who support me routinely with their advice, stories, and expertise. I couldn't do this without you.

# PHOTO CREDITS

## FIGURE CAPTIONS

01fig01: Images © iStock
01fig02: Image courtesy MindMeister.com
05fig01: (No photo credit needed)
05fig02: Images © iStock
05fig03: (No photo credit needed)
05fig04: Custom frame © Joanne Sharpe
06fig01: Images © iStock
06fig02: Images © iStock
06fig03: Images © iStock
06fig04: Images © iStock

06fig05: Images © iStock
07fig01: Images © iStock
07fig02: Images © iStock
08fig01: Images © iStock
08fig02: Images © iStock
08fig03: Images © iStock
09fig01: Images © iStock
09fig02: Images © iStock
10fig01: Images © iStock
10fig02: Images © iStock
11fig01: Images © iStock
11fig02: Images © iStock
12fig01: Images © iStock
12fig02: Images © iStock
13fig01: Images © iStock
14fig01: Images © iStock
14fig02: Images © iStock
15fig01: Images © iStock
15fig02: Images © iStock
16fig01: Images © iStock
19fig01: Images © iStock
20fig01: Images courtesy StepOneVisionBoards.com
20fig02: Images courtesy StepOneVisionBoards.com
20fig03: Images © iStock
20fig04: Images courtesy StepOneVisionBoards.com
21fig01: Images © iStock
21fig02: Images © iStock
INfig01: Images © iStock
INfig02: Images © iStock
INfig03: Images © iStock
INfig04: Images © iStock

INfig05: Images © iStock
INfig06: Images © iStock
INfig07: Images © iStock
INfig08: Images © iStock

## ABOUT THE AUTHOR

Marcia Layton Turner is a bestselling, award-winning author who has used visualization techniques for years to achieve her dreams. After reading the blockbuster book *The Secret*,

Marcia researched vision boards as a tool for goal setting and success. Later she taught a class in creating and using vision boards for greater career, financial, relationship, and spiritual success.

Marcia's credits include *Woman's Day,* Forbes.com, *Businessweek, Entrepreneur, Black Enterprise,* and many others. She has also authored, coauthored, or ghost-written more than forty other books about marketing, entrepreneurship, and real estate.

Marcia earned a bachelor's degree with honors from Wellesley College and an MBA from the University of Michigan.